1499

Making Senses Out of Scripture

Making Senses Out of Scripture

Reading the Bible As the First Christians Did

Mark P. Shea

Basilica Press
SAN DIEGO

www.basilicapress.com
800-933-9398

Cover design by Charlotte Johnson
99 00 01 02 03 15 14 13 12 11 10 09 08 07 06 05 04 03 02 01

Printed in the United States of America ∞
ISBN 0-9642610-6-5

Basilica Press is a division of the Missionaries of Faith Foundation.

Contents

To my Mom

Littera gesta docet
Quid credas allegoria
Moralis quid agas
Quo tendis anagogia

The letter speaks of deeds.
Allegory to faith.
The moral how to act.
Anagogy our destiny.

— Augustine of Dacia

Foreword

Growing up Catholic, I got a healthy dose of Scripture at every mass. As a youngster, the great events of Scripture such as the fall of Adam and Eve, the Exodus, David and Goliath, and the journeys of the apostle Paul were familiar to me. And though the stories did not "hang together" as a single story, still they stirred my interest and grabbed my imagination. As a result of my parents faithfully exposing me to the "pure milk of the word" week in and week out, my hunger for truth grew slowly but surely, though not without its obstacles — obstacles faced by many a Catholic who has wondered about the Bible and wanted to know more of it.

When I was confirmed, my parents gave me a beautiful, black leather Bible. It was a St. Joseph edition complete with gilded pages and beautiful pictures. I remember that first night like it was yesterday. I placed the precious Bible on my bedstand and stared at it, thinking about all those stories I'd heard were contained in this book. I was excited at the thought that this holy book, which I was accustomed to seeing only in mass, was now in my bedroom. I was drawn to it as if it contained the secrets of the universe.

I opened the book that night with great anticipation, like Indiana Jones upon discovering a rare and secret document. Determined to read that entire Bible, I started with one verse per night. After about three weeks, my adventure ground to a halt. I could not make sense of the stories.

I needed someone to assist me. That Bible sat for several years amidst the other great books on my full bookshelf. But though it was gathering dust on the shelf, it was gathering momentum in my heart until the day the dust was blown off it by a young lady named Emily (who was later to become my wife).

Emily described to me how God spoke to her through Scripture. As she did, my interest in discovering the truths of the Bible was rekindled. For the next three weeks after Emily and I talked, I raced over to her house after school and sat at the kitchen table, intently listening to her mother teach me from the Book. My eyes, as if at a ping pong match, went from her mother to the open Bible and back to her mother. I thought, "This Bible is not just a surface story! There are many *levels* of meaning there! But how do I come to know and understand them?"

The excitement and joy of Emily's mother as she explained Scripture was enough to get me to read the Bible with a renewed sense of hope that I too could understand it. I pored over the entire text many times, each time discovering new insights. This book was like no other I had ever read. I could not exhaust its treasures and the more I learned, the more I realized how little I knew.

My journey eventually took me out of the Catholic Church, where I pastored Protestant churches for twelve years. As an independent pastor, I fell into the subjective pattern of interpreting scripture. There was no established rule of interpretation, no riverbanks in which the waters of revelation could flow. Upon my return to the Catholic Church, I discovered how her rich heritage provides great freedom in Scripture study, while lending sound guidance in making sense out of the text. I have been both overjoyed and amazed by the depth of Scripture discoverable in the light of the living Tradition of the Church.

Pope John Paul II says in *Crossing The Threshold of Hope*, "The history of salvation is very simple." This is true. In one sense, you can spend a few hours enjoying the thrill of grasping the big picture of what God has done in Christ. Yet while the story is "simple," it is not shallow. You can spend a lifetime discovering its deep mysteries.

In *Making Senses Out of Scripture*, Mark Shea gives us a great gift. Not only does he provide a summary of the grand sweep of salvation history, he explains in everyday language the keys to discovering the different senses of scripture: that is, going beyond the surface to the deeper meanings of Scripture. In this volume, Mark provides actual examples of how this is done, making the book a great source for individual as well as group study. As I have used many of Mark's insights from his previous books (*By What Authority?* and *This is My Body*), so this book will also become one of my sources for encouraging others in Scripture study. For the hungry in heart, you will be fed. For those who have been reading the Bible for years and still want more, open wide. You will not be disappointed.

—*Jeff Cavins*

Acknowledgements

Thanks above all to God, the Father, Son and Holy Spirit, from Whom, to Whom and through Whom this book and all things exist. Blessed be He!

Thanks also to Janet, my wife, for her patience with me during the long days I was squirrelled away at the keyboard. Also, to our boys, Luke, Matthew, Peter and Sean, of whom I am so proud. I love you all.

Deep gratitude also goes to Dr. Scott Hahn, who suggested the idea for this book and who has been a steady advocate and friend throughout its gestation and birth.

Thanks to Jeff Cavins, for your kind words and your patience with the constantly ringing phone.

In addition, heaps o'thanks go to:

The Missionaries of Faith Foundation (and in particular Daniel Daou) whose vision for reacquainting the members of the Church with Sacred Scripture is wonderfully exciting! May God bless the work of your hands!

The people of Blessed Sacrament parish in Seattle, Washington: Thanks for being home.

All my friends at the Catherine of Siena Institute in Seattle. You guys do awesome work!

Mike Aquilina: A good friend, a good editor, and a great Catholic.

J. S. Bach, The Montreux Band, Darol Anger, Mike Marshall, Pat Metheny, Phil Keaggy and Nightnoise: musicians whose beauty helped me write.

Johnnette Benkovic: For her interest in this project.

G. K. Chesterton: Still my hero.

Cat Clark: Magnificent Muse of Researchers.

Dave Curp: Historian Extraordinaire, Beloved Brother, and provider of what almost amount to foreign language footnotes that lend my work a veneer of respectibility.

Nancy Custer: Dear friend and enthusiastic supporter.

Marcus Grodi: A friend who knows the way Home.

C. S. Lewis: Yet another of my heroes.

Steve Kellmeyer: author of the invaluable book *Scriptural Catholicism*.

Michael and Ivy Lounsbery: For variously acting as prayer partner and crack research squad.

Steve Ray: Profound gratitude for your enthusiastic support!

A special thanks to Patrick Madrid, Fearless Editor, for getting this book seaworthy.

Also special thanks to Saints Jerome, Athanasius, Anthony of the Desert, Francis de Sales, Dominic and Tertius, on whose constant intercession I relied for help. *Ora pro nobis.*

Introduction

Confessions of a Failed
Pioneer in Biblical Studies

It is fools, they say, who learn by experience. But since they do at last learn, let a fool bring his experience into the common stock that wiser men may profit by it.
— C. S. Lewis

When I was about thirteen years old my brother got hold of a brittle old King James Bible that had belonged to his wife's grandparents. It was published in the 1840s and its pages were yellow and dry as dust, with exceptionally small print.

I had no church background whatsoever, and my only familiarity with Holy Writ was based on watching *The Robe* at Easter and *A Charlie Brown Christmas* at Christmastime. Beyond that, I had a vague impression of togas, creepy prophecies, angels, "The Lord is my Shepherd," dire threats about Hell, "Love one another" and snatches of "Away in a Manger", but that was about it. What was this mysterious Book that everybody has been talking about for so long? I decided to find out. So I plunged in and began reading Genesis, Chapter 1, Verse 1, determined to plow through until I got to the book of Revelation.

My resolve held firm and I nearly made it — to Genesis, Chapter 4. But when I got to the bit about the talking snake, I'd seen enough. Whatever this book was, it didn't square up too well with my thirteen-year-old understanding of Science and History. And besides, it was kinda boring, the print was hard to read and the language was old-fashioned.

So I ruffled around through the pages (not having the foggiest idea where to try again) until I remembered that Revelation was supposed to be a pretty wild book. I'd seen some very creepy pamphlets (crammed into my Halloween bag by Fundamentalists concerned for my little soul) written by some guy named Jack Chick. He loved to illustrate scary, lurid stuff about The Antichrist and The Coming World Upheaval and this had given me a spooky thrill as I'd munched on my Butterfingers and Tootsie Rolls after trick-or-treating. Also I'd seen something on TV about ancient astronauts helping inspire the biblical prophets (who mistook their interplanetary saucers for heavenly visions). And I believed in clairvoyance because my pal in middle school had some spooky dreams once. So I figured I was a good candidate to read Revelation and Figure It All Out, given my intellectual superiority over the primitive unscientific people who had written nonsense like Genesis.

Once again, therefore, I plunged in and made my way for a while through the angels, plagues, battles, and beasts. I was taken aback by the thought of Jesus with a sword sticking out of his mouth. I was grossed out by the description of a Lamb with seven eyes. I gave up when it came to the part about the Number of the Beast. I had figured I'd be able to work it out because I was pretty good at puzzles. But I couldn't.

"Weird book," I shrugged. I put it down and did not read it again until I became a Christian at the age of twenty.

Why I Picked Up the Bible Again

When I was twenty years old, I went to college, but I did not get the education I thought I was going to get. Instead, I had an encounter with the living God. It happened this way:

First, without my going to church or reading a Bible or studying theology, I came face-to-face with my own capacity for sin and evil. I discovered I could use people and discard them like trash. I discovered I had little idea of what love was. I discovered I was a venal, selfish excuse for a human being. I discovered, in short, that I had sinned, through my own fault.

Second, at the same time I was discovering these unpleasant facts about myself, I was coming to know a group of Evangelical Christians who lived on my dormitory floor. They were very attractive people. Where I had murk, they had light. Where I had confusion, they had clarity. Where I had torment, they had peace. Where I had selfishness, they had love. And where I had sin, they had mercy.

I had, in the years since I put down that King James Bible, been socialized to dismiss Christians as ignoramuses and wahoos. My encounter with the Bible had assisted me in forming this prejudice, but the real root of it was simply the desire not to be a nerd in high school. Christians were uncool, and coolness was the brass ring on the merry-go-round of high school life, so I had given Christians a wide berth. Now, however, with my pride in tatters, I began to reassess that opinion. I furtively listened to their "God talk." I watched Franco Zeffirelli's *Jesus of Nazareth* with them (and was deeply moved by it). I saw several curious and spooky answers to prayer. I saw their genuine love.

I read Chuck Colson's *Born Again* and C. S. Lewis' *Mere Christianity*. And I began to revisit the Bible, especially the gospels, which I now read for the first time.

It was Lewis who helped me the most during that time. Till I read *Mere Christianity*, my grasp of the Bible was in pretty much the state it had been when I was thirteen: just a few bits of images and mental flotsam I had no idea how to organize. In a few pages, Lewis sketched the relationship of the Old and New Testaments so that I got the big picture. From there, I could begin to see how the parts of the Bible related to the whole and how the message of Christ emerged out of it in a coherent way. He showed me the skeletal structure of Scripture.

But in addition to Lewis, many years of Bible study, teaching, prayer, and fellowship at my local church were necessary for me to really put flesh and blood on that skeleton. With the help of the group of Christians on my dorm floor, I came to encounter Jesus Christ through his word in a living way and to discover with new eyes the truth of Scripture. I owe them an unpayable debt.

But I also learned from them a deeply mistaken notion. For within a few months of my accepting Christ as Lord and Savior, I had incorporated into my outlook a sort of offhand belief which flatly contradicted not only my own experience but common sense: namely, I had adopted a blithe certainty that Scripture was simple, clear, and obvious to all, and that anyone can just pick it up and understand it lickety-split. Given my previous history, you would think I would have noticed the irony. For, in fact, I had gone from one extreme to another; from the notion that Scripture was utterly incomprehensible to the notion that Scripture was so crystal clear that I, alone and without the help of anyone else, could master its depths.

But I didn't notice the irony. Instead I continued for about seven years, both learning about the Bible with the aid of other Christians and yet, curiously enough, imagining "Scripture alone" was sufficient for me to discern the revelation of God. Then something happened that brought me back to reality. To tell you that story, let me tell you another one first.

Not Exactly the Gift of Tongues

One cold Michigan day when I was six years old, I was out playing in the carport and began to get thirsty. Noticing a thick layer of frost on the bumper of our Buick got me thinking. Frost is water, I reasoned. So right then and there, I decided to lick the frost off that bumper. . .

Being trapped in a squat with your tongue stuck fast to the freezing bumper of a Buick can be a philosophically nourishing experience. You embark on trains of thought that can lead to

- a beneficial revelation of one's own ignorance (*"I didn't know this would happen."*)

- a newfound respect for the experience of others, particularly elders (*"I wonder if I'm the only one this ever happened to. Maybe I should have talked to Mom and Dad before I did this."*)

- a new appreciation of the need for practical guidance (*"How do I get my tongue off this bumper?"*)

- a deepened awareness of the struggle of humility vs. pride (*"What'll I do if someone sees me? On the other hand, what if they don't?"*)

- and a renewed reverence for wisdom won by painful experience (*"If I ever have kids, I gonna make sure this never happens to them."*)

As with the mute man Jesus healed, my tongue was eventually loosed (by a sharp jerk of my head), and I too "told no one" (talking was a bit painful for a few days). Instead, I, er, held my tongue and pondered all these things in my heart — for a time.

Fast forward to the mid-1980s. My encounter with the Buick is a faded memory. I am now living in the curious dichotomy of believing "The Bible Alone" is sufficient to know the revelation of Christ, yet depending each and every day on my church, my teachers, radio programs, books and TV shows to help me penetrate the mysteries of the word. I have absorbed enough Evangelicalism into my blood by now to fancy that Sacred Tradition is an authoritarian affair imposed on Christians by the Catholic Church to keep Christians from the plain Word of God. Far better, I was taught, to be "Spirit-led." To be Spirit-led was to leave "human wisdom" behind and dwell in the region where we *genuinely* met God. The Spirit-led life (I was told) is spontaneous, unpredictable and creative as the Catholic Church is stodgy and flat-footed. It is personal as Sacred Tradition is impersonal; authentic as Sacred Tradition is artificial; truly of the heart as Sacred Tradition is merely of the head.

"So," said I, "We have the Bible and God is all-powerful and able to lead us by his Spirit. Who needs Tradition and Church? The Word is simple!" How quickly I'd forgotten that thirteen-year-old kid, his King James Bible, and all the people who'd eventually helped him understand it.

The trouble came with a little book by an author who I later discovered to be what theologians call an extreme Calvinist. He was a cheery fellow who agreed that Scripture is all you need. He agreed that God is all-powerful (Scripture says he's all-powerful, doesn't it?). Well, said our friend, if he's *all*-powerful, then he's *so* powerful he chooses *everything* — right down to whether or not you will go to Heaven or Hell (or didn't I *believe* he's really *all*-powerful like the Bible says?). Therefore, said our friend, your chance of heaven has nothing whatsoever to do with what *you* want. If God decides it, then in his all-powerful will you'll make it. It'll be irresistible. But if (for reasons of his own) God *doesn't* want you, you'll simply *have* to sin, be damned and end up in Hell because God (who is, you recall, *all*-powerful) *wanted* you to go there before you were born. It's right there in Scripture, said our cheery Calvinist (and here he gave a string of biblical references that seemed to strongly support his argument). And, he concluded with a twist of the knife, if all this seemed to me appallingly ugly, unjust and immoral, God's reply was simplicity itself: "O man, who art thou that repliest against God? Shall the thing formed say to him who formed it, Why has thou made me thus?" (Romans 9:20). In short, my inability to appreciate our friend's picture of God was a sign that *I* had not experienced Irresistible Grace and was therefore, sooner or later, destined to be damned. Case closed.

It is difficult to exaggerate the devastating impact this little book had on me. The church that I belonged to at this time taught nothing like this. It always emphasized our capacity to choose. We held regular altar calls, and were right at home with all the normal Evangelical talk about "making a decision for Christ and accepting Jesus as your personal Lord and Savior." Over and over it was stressed that God desired the salvation of *all* and that the only reason a person could not be saved was because they did not *want* to be saved. Now I was suddenly being presented with Scriptural passages that seemed to argue quite strongly that *God* does not want all to be saved. Moreover, I was being told by my little book that Christians (such as my little Evangelical church) who spoke of "free will" were "twisting Scripture" or taking it out of context. I thought the portrait of God offered by my little Calvinist book was unspeakably ugly but I was fearful that it was giving the "objective Scriptural picture" whereas I was merely believing what my itching ears wanted to hear. How was I supposed to sort it out?

So there I was, thirsty for Living Water yet somehow I had gotten my tongue stuck to a freezing Calvinist bumper. It was one thing to vaguely worship a God whose unpredictability signaled a wonderful creative flair. It was quite another to be presented with a God whose unpredictability signaled a Cosmic Psychopathic Complex. Everything I had believed about God looked as though it must collapse before this convincing horror. After all, it seemed to have all the earmarks: it was simple and it seemed scriptural. What was I to do?

The answer to this and other difficulties I was beginning to have with the idea of "The Bible Alone" lay in the lesson I had learned long ago in that carport: realize I got into this jam because of ignorance and look to wiser heads to help me get out of it and avoid it in the future. For though I was the first one in my young church to encounter this doctrine, I was not, I discovered, the first one in history. The Catholic Church, from Augustine to the present day, had chewed the problem over with a lot of thought and Spirit-led prayer (hundreds of years *more* thought and prayer than I would ever be *alive*) and had discovered some rather respectable answers to my Calvinist friend. I discovered that others long before me had taken Scripture as seriously as me and had believed in the Spirit's guidance as much as I did. They worked slowly and painfully through *all* of Scripture, listening to what the Fathers, Doctors and great theologians of the Church have said. They dealt with *all* the data rather than leaping to the conclusions of my little Calvinist book. And eventually, after long rumination, the Church stated its conclusions about this and many other equally thorny questions via the teaching of the councils, encyclicals and so forth.[1] In short, I found the teaching office or Magisterium of the Church had done its homework so that schlemiels like me wouldn't have to reinvent the

---

[1] Conclusions based on the fact that God's all-powerful will is expressed not by making us puppets, but by making us free (as he is free). That is why St. Paul says, "Where the Spirit of the Lord is, there is freedom" (2 Corinthians 3:17). Thus, we are free either to embrace God (and with him joy, power, love and peace) or to reject him and get exactly what we ask for. But God himself wills the salvation of all, not the irresistible salvation of some and the irresistible sin and damnation of others. As the *Catechism of the Catholic Church* (no. 605) says, "At the end of the parable of the lost sheep Jesus recalled that God's love excludes no one: 'So it is not the will of your Father who is in heaven that one of these little ones should perish.' He affirms that he came 'to give his life as a ransom for many'; this last term is not restrictive, but contrasts the whole of humanity with the unique person of the redeemer who hands himself over to save us. The Church, following the apostles, teaches that Christ died for all men without exception: 'There is not, never has been, and never will be a single human being for whom Christ did not suffer.' "

wheel every time somebody came up with a convincing yet insane new theory about God.

So, in the end, I came to admit that to be led by the Holy Spirit in the real world with its imbalances and excesses is to be led *toward* Sacred Tradition and the Church, not away from them.[2] My demand that Bible study be simple in a world like ours was, to quote G. K. Chesterton,

> exactly as if somebody were to say about the science of medicine: "All I ask is Health; what could be simpler than the beautiful gift of Health? Why not be content to enjoy for ever the glow of youth and the fresh enjoyment of being fit? Why study dry and dismal sciences of anatomy and physiology; why inquire about the whereabouts of obscure organs of the human body? Why pedantically distinguish between what is labeled a poison and what is labeled an antidote, when it is so simple to enjoy Health?"[3]

In short then, just as my adolescent rejection of the Bible had been simplistic, so my insistence on Me and the Bible Alone was simplistic too. The Bible, like a Michigan winter morning, is a beautiful thing, not something to reject as impossible to understand like a thirteen-year-old boy I know once did. But it is also, like a Michigan winter morning, a difficult and even dangerous thing full of unexpected wonders. . . and freezing Buick bumpers. It is not simple, easy, or obvious. It is as strange, complex and beautiful as the human body, for it is the anatomical manual of the Body of Christ.

---

[2] For a fuller history of my change of mind concerning the merits of Sacred Tradition, see my *By What Authority?: An Evangelical Discovers Catholic Tradition* (Huntington: Our Sunday Visitor Books, 1996).

[3] G. K. Chesterton, *The Thing: Why I Am a Catholic*, (New York: Dodd, Mead & Co., 1930).

There are, then, two very basic wrong ways to study the Bible, just as there are two very basic wrong ways to study medicine. The first wrong way is to not study it at all. The second is to study it as though we were the Lone Ranger or the first doctor to ever wonder what was hidden beneath our skin. Happily, we are not the first. God has provided us with wise "Doctors of the Church" who have gone before us and mapped out the anatomical structure of Revelation in the common life, common worship and common teaching of the Body of Christ. That map is Sacred Tradition in its written and unwritten form and the mapmakers are the saints, theologians, philosophers and biblical scholars in union with the Magisterium — the living teaching office of the Church. These three things together — Tradition, Scripture, and Magisterium — are an unbeatable combination, a combination the Catholic Church alone has in its fullness. They give Scripture its healthy and proper context and help us to see just how it can be fruitfully applied to our lives.

Given that Scripture exists in this larger context of the common life, teaching, and worship of the Church, this book will try to sketch that context a little bit and give some basic tools for reading Scripture as Christians have historically done. The book will therefore be laid out as follows:

Part I: The Big Picture

The first section of this book consists of Chapters 1 through 5. In this section, we will set biblical revelation between its two bookends: that is, natural revelation (i.e., what we can tell about God by looking around at stuff) and the Magisterium (i.e., the teaching office of the Church created by Christ when he gave Peter and the apostles and their successors, the Pope and bishops, the authority to conserve and interpret his revelation in written and unwritten Tradition).

- Chapter 1 will examine natural revelation and see how it prepares us for the supernatural revelation which begins to unfold in the Old Testament.

- Chapters 2 and 3 do a sort of fly-over of the Old Testament story, highlighting the covenants with Adam, Noah, Abraham, Moses and David and showing how all these prefigure and anticipate the new and final covenant in Christ. "Why a fly-over? Why not more in-depth?" you ask? Because this is a book aimed at helping *you* learn to read the Bible, and if I do it for you I'll ruin the fun! Therefore we will only be skimming the mountaintops of revelation so you can get the general lay of the Old Testament land. It will fall to you, gentle reader, to parachute down into the lowlands once you have closed this book. But don't worry. You'll be adequately provisioned to start that journey by the time we are done.

- Once we have done the fly-over of the Old Testament, Chapter 4 will move on to briefly discuss a) what God was up to beyond the land of Israel, b) how he providentially arranged things among the Gentiles to intertwine with his work of revelation in the Old Testament, and c) the New Testament evidence that this very God, "in the fullness of time" was conceived of the Holy Spirit, born of the Virgin Mary, and became man in the person of an obscure carpenter living in a backwater village on the fringe of the Roman Empire: Jesus of Nazareth.

• In Chapter 5, we will pass from discussing who Jesus is to what he did and show how his person and work shed light on all previous revelation, as well as discuss how all previous revelation has him mysteriously hidden within it.

Part II: The Four Senses of Scripture

Once this overview of revelation is complete, we will then do a sort of "post-game wrap up" in which we look at the *way* in which we have been reading Scripture in the previous five chapters. As we do, we will examine how, in the New Testament and in the Catholic Tradition of biblical study that springs from it, there are classically four senses of Scripture: namely, the literal, allegorical, moral, and anagogical senses.

What the heck are those, you ask? Ah, a rich feast, my Bible-hungry friend! Read on. You'll be glad you did.

PART I

The Big Picture

1

The *Myst*-ery of Revelation

*Created in God's image and called to know and love him,
the person who seeks God discovers certain ways of coming
to know him. These are also called proofs for the existence
of God, not in the sense of proofs in the natural sciences,
but rather in the sense of "converging and convincing arguments," which allow us to attain certainty about the
truth.*

*These "ways" of approaching God from creation have
a twofold point of departure: the physical world and the
human person.*

— Catechism of the Catholic Church, no. 31

This past Christmas my kids got a computer game called
Myst. It is a very curious game. There are no instructions,
no rules, and no commentary offered at the beginning of
the game. You find yourself plunked down into a strange
and unknown environment on a mysterious island. You do
not know where you are and you do not know why you
are there. As you look around, you discover various things
that were put there before you by some unseen intelligence.
There are rocks, trees, buildings, books, and many other

things and they are invested with a mysterious, disjointed, and elusive significance. Push this button, and a map appears. But you don't know what the map portrays. Open that door, and there is a strange machine which hums and "works" at the flip of a switch but you have no idea what it does. You open various books, and the books tell fragments of stories, but you don't know what the stories are about. You go to various buildings and examine various pieces of furniture and different objects. You know what they are, you even know that they must mean something, but you don't know what that meaning might be.

As you keep playing, you begin to discover connections between the strange paraphernalia you stumble upon. You find a book showing a piano keyboard and giving instructions to play a certain sequence of notes. Then you discover just such a keyboard elsewhere on the island. So, of course, you play the notes to see what happens. (I won't tell you what happens because I don't want to spoil the game for you.)

As you can imagine, in such a mysterious world everything becomes charged with great significance. There's no telling what some seemingly trivial thing you run across might signify. You have the sense that you are always moving in the precincts of a great mystery. You become increasingly convinced that there is some master key that can make sense of the connections between things in this world. You begin to feel that the connections, though mysterious, are not random.

Now in a curious way, revelation proceeds in a way similar to the game of *Myst*. We do not start out as adults with Bibles giving us a full set of instructions for the rules of the game, but as children with eyes, ears, noses, tongues, fingers, heads, and especially, hearts. And through these portals come the first streams of light by which the "dawn from on high shall break upon us" (Luke 1:78). It was the same in the childhood of the world. The earliest civilizations did not have the benefit of a written revelation. God permitted most of humanity to muddle along for quite a while simply "feeling for him" as St. Paul said (Acts 17:27) on much the same basis as a non-Christian or a child today might do. He is not afraid to allow himself to be revealed in the childhood of the world (and to the childlike heart today) through what he has made. And so, we come to know about God first of all by looking around.

Some people are surprised to discover that the Bible itself teaches this. St. Paul tells us that God's primal revelation comes not through prophets or holy writings or mystical visions, but simply through the created stuff we see every day.

> For what can be known about God is plain to them, because God has shown it to them. Ever since the creation of the world his invisible nature, namely, his eternal power and deity, has been clearly perceived in the things that have been made. (Romans 1:19–20)

That is, God has made it possible to know that he exists, that he is almighty and that he is Creator of all things, not by "blind faith" but just by looking around at things with an unprejudiced heart. It is well to understand this, for such "pre-biblical" revelation sets the stage for biblical revelation. So let us consider it briefly and note that the natural (as distinct from supernatural) evidence for God is presented to us every day in the form of two basic things: the physical world and the human person.

The Physical World

Babies come from mommies and daddies, cars come from builders and engineers, and trees come from acorns. And though little children may simply rest content with that explanation, adults inevitably ask, "Where do the parents, builders and acorns come from?" And so we find that everything participates in a "Great Chain of Being" which takes us further and further into the past until we get to the Big Bang itself. Absolutely nothing in Nature is unhooked from that chain. Everything in *this* universe is caused by something *else* in this universe which is caused by something else in this universe and so on and so on and scoobie doobie doobie. Our awareness of this is so fundamental that when something *does* break that Chain of Being (as, for instance, the miracle of the loaves and fishes does in John 6:1–14), we have to find an explanation for it by either saying, as Catholics do, that the God who exists outside Nature added some links to the Chain, or else we must say, as skeptics do, that it has some sort of natural cause (i.e., people sharing lunches, or a big lie by the apostles who were, so to speak, yanking our great Chain of Being). The one thing nobody believes in is what philosopher Peter Kreeft calls the "Pop Theory"[1] — that things like loaves and fishes just pop into existence for no reason at all. They must have a cause, either natural (i.e., bakers and fish eggs) or supernatural, (i.e. direct creation by God the Creator). Nothing in this world can cause itself to exist. Every created thing relies on some thing ahead of it to pull it into

---

[1] Peter Kreeft, *Fundamentals of the Faith: Essays in Christian Apologetics*, (San Francisco: Ignatius, 1988), p. 29.

being, just as a boxcar relies on the car ahead of it to pull it uphill.

Very well then, if existence is like a big train going uphill, we have to ask, "What is the Engine?" We can't say that there is some break in the chain — that some natural thing just popped itself into existence fifteen billion years ago — just as we can't say that loaves and fishes just popped themselves into existence 2,000 years ago. Hence, appeals to the Big Bang don't explain away God. They just say that some unthinkable Power that is not the Universe itself caused the Universe to exist (because the Universe itself, like the teeny weeny things that comprise it [such as loaves and fishes], has not the power to make itself exist). Therefore, there must be some sort of Uncaused Cause beyond the natural universe. And that, as St. Thomas says, is what everybody means by "God."[2] So from looking around, we can infer that God exists, just as St. Paul says.

Likewise, from looking around, we can infer that God *designs*. So, for instance, when we see a microcomputer, we say "The hand of a designer was here." When we see the fathomlessly greater complexity of the human brain that made the microcomputer, we similarly respond, "The Hand of a Designer was here."[3] Likewise, when we look at the sheer scope, scale, terror and wonder of the universe in which we find ourselves, we conclude that whatever else

---

[2] St. Thomas Aquinas, *Summa Theologiae*, I, 2, 3.

[3] And, increasingly, so do thinkers and scientists such as Michael Behe (*Darwin's Black Box: The Biochemical Challenge to Evolution*) and Philip Johnson (*Darwin on Trial*) and Hugh Ross (*The Creator and the Cosmos*). So, of course, did St. Thomas Aquinas in his *Summa Theologiae* (Part I, Question 2, Article 3).

may be true about the Maker and Designer behind such a universe, it is infinitely powerful as well as infinitely ingenious. In other words, the complexity and the vastness of creation betokens God's "eternal power and deity" as St. Paul says. This is exactly why most of the world has always been religious, not atheistic. Like any good *Myst* player, the average man, woman, or child can connect the dots. They're not so arrogant as to suppose they know much about the mysterious Power that made the world. But neither are they such fools as to gaze upon a cosmos pregnant with such meaning, design, and sheer wonder and attribute it to Nothing. It takes more dogged faith than most people can muster to be an atheist.

The Human Person

But, of course, being religious can mean almost anything. Indeed, based on the data we have looked at so far, many people can and do conclude that the power behind the Universe is something impersonal, like the Force in *Star Wars*. Such a view of God (technically known as pantheism) is an ancient opinion which is particularly popular in the West these days because, as an atheist acquaintance said, it is a bit like spiritual methadone treatment. It gives you the pleasures of religious faith without any of the troubling demands. In the words of C. S. Lewis,

> An "impersonal God" — well and good. A subjective God of beauty, truth and goodness inside our own heads — better still. A formless life force surging through us, a vast power which we can tap — best of all. . . . The Pantheist's

God does nothing, demands nothing. He is there if you wish for Him, like a book on a shelf. He will not pursue you.[4]

Pantheism essentially tells us that God is identical with Creation. And, of course, if God is Everything then we are considerably relieved of the burden of having to choose between right and wrong, good and evil.

The trouble with pantheism is that it tries to make God something "beyond personal" but instead winds up calling God something *less* than personal. Many people harbor in the back of their minds the notion they are being "truly spiritual" when they say "We must get rid of the crude fancies of the puny human mind with its primitive agricultural images of shepherds, sheep, vineyards and all the rest of it. We must instead thrust our spirits into contact with a realm beyond the imagination!" Nine times out of ten, what this means in practice is abandoning older and more nourishing religious symbols for newer and more impoverished ones. It usually means picturing God as an invisible gas or energy field, to cite enormously popular sci-fi imagery. And the explanation for this is simple. It is not that the energy field devotee has a higher religious consciousness. It is simply that he or she has, like most people in a technological society, known things like magnetism or electricity as their closest experiences of invisible power.

But the reality is that neither gas nor electric sparks nor magnets are terribly interesting conversationalists. A long

---

[4] C.S. Lewis, *Miracles* (New York: Macmillan, 1947), pp. 93–94.

chat with a magnet will yield few wise insights whether we are pantheists or Christians. And this is our clue that we have made a wrong turn in shooting for something impersonal as the Ultimate Reality. For it turns out that we contemplate magnets and gases far more often than they contemplate us. It turns out, in short, that the average man, woman and child seem to have a much more vast and varied mind, heart and soul than most magnets, gases or electric sparks. And for this reason we can say there exists something in this world that is more than mere "Creation" — more even than magnetic and gaseous creation — though it is most certainly a creature as well.

That something is the human person, and every attempt to reduce humans to equality with mere nature is doomed to failure. Some who try to do so note, for instance, that humans share many common physical traits with the beasts as though this made humans equal to beasts. The problem with this argument is that human beings alone in all the cosmos are aware of and interested in the fact of our similarity with our fellow creatures. Not one other critter in the world recognizes it because not one other critter in the world is capable of reason as human beings are. Cats do not rhapsodize about their brotherhood with mice. Oak trees seldom hug environmentalists. And great apes do not concern themselves with tracing the evolutionary evidence of their common ancestry with us. These are purely human activities, conducted by human persons who, alone in all the natural world, can see and reason about such matters — because they alone are endowed with reason in all the natural world.

Likewise, humans are distinguishable from all of natural

Creation in their ability to see and create beauty. In the words of G. K. Chesterton, "Art is the signature of man."[5] We do not find rough studies of how a wildebeest swings its head sketched in the dirt by the chimpanzees of Africa. Those creatures biologically nearest us in the great dynasties of the animal kingdom — the primates — are still so remotely different from us that there exists an unbridgeable chasm between our capacity to create and theirs. Such creativity and love of beauty does not square well with the attempt to claim that there is no real difference between humans and other creatures. It does, however, make a remarkable amount of sense in light of the biblical account of humans as somehow being made in the image of God who creates. And so, looking not merely at Creation-in-general, but at the strange creature called *homo sapiens*, we can begin to glimpse, not only that God is, but that, if Man and Woman are any reflection of him, he may just be more like an artist than an energy field or a gas.

Looking at the human person shows us other things as well, particularly because we *are* human beings, not just "impartial observers" looking *at* human beings. When we see this we begin to notice something besides creativity: namely, morality.

A modern reader will almost surely snort at this word. If human beings are so moral, why do they act like such dirtbags so often? The problem, however, only highlights the central point. For though we complain strenuously that a man is evil if he kills, dismembers and eats a child, we

---

[5] G. K. Chesterton, *The Everlasting Man* (Garden City: Image, 1955), p. 34.

do not similarly complain if a crocodile does this. In both cases, the same thing happens, but in the former case we recognize that the man is acting contrary to his true nature as a moral agent while in the latter case the crocodile is *not* a moral agent, but simply a creature of instinct. The crocodile is not "to blame" as a man is to blame for his act. The moment we recognize this (and only those lobotomized by trendy philosophical fads do not recognize it), we recognize that there is a component to human makeup not present in other creatures: the awareness of justice. Indeed, the essence of the complaint against "dirtbags" is that they treat others, not like people, but like lesser created things. That is, they are unjust and we know it.

And so we complain of the man who treats a woman like a "sex object" and not a person. We fault employers who treat their employees "like dogs" and not persons. And we rightly condemn the Nazis for butchering Jews and Slavs "like animals" and not respecting them like persons. In all these things, even human evil shows that humans are different than the rest of Creation. Even in their distorted and evil acts, they image something of God that cannot be seen by contemplating the rest of the created order. For the demand of conscience shows, both in the breach and the observance, that humans are aware of some higher demand enjoined upon them for justice and common decency. When that demand is honored by human beings, they take care to respect and even love their neighbors in ways which could never occur to beasts. On the other hand, when they are determined to ignore this demand upon conscience, they can create evils no animal would ever think to perpetrate. Our race is related to other creatures on this planet like a race of gods, says Chesterton, and "the fact is not lessened but emphasised because it can behave like a race of demons."[6]

So we come to the end of this quick survey of what can be known about God just by looking around. "God," says theologian Scott Hahn, " 'writes' the world like men write words, to convey truth and love. So nature and history are more than just created things — God fashions them as visible signs of other things, uncreated realities, which are eternal and invisible."[7] And we can know those things by the light of our natural reason without prophetic bells and whistles or voices out of the sky. All we need is the sense God gave a goose.

The problem however, is that we are not always able to have even that much sense. In the words of Pope Pius XII:

> The human reason is, strictly speaking, truly capable by its own natural power and light of attaining to a true and certain knowledge of the one personal God, who watches over and controls the world by his providence, and of the natural law written on our hearts by the Creator; yet there are many obstacles which prevent reason from the effective and fruitful use of this inborn faculty. For the truths that concern the relations between God and man wholly transcend the visible order of things, and, if they are translated into human action and influence it, they call for self-surrender and abnegation. The human mind, in its turn, is hampered in the attaining of such truths, not only by the impact of the senses and the imagination, but

---

[6] Chesterton, *The Everlasting Man*, p. 268.

[7] Scott Hahn, *A Father Who Keeps His Promises*, (Ann Arbor: Servant, 1998), p. 22.

also by disordered appetites which are the consequences of original sin. So it happens that men in such matters easily persuade themselves that what they would not like to be true is false or at least doubtful.[8]

Thus, in the discovery of our capacity for evil, we necessarily discover the flaw in the "instrument" through which we are looking at God: namely, the cracked and dirty lens of our own fallen human existence. There is something *wrong* with us, which is why we snort and complain about humans being "dirtbags" (and why we ourselves hang back reluctantly at the ominous words "self-surrender" and "abnegation"). We can see *some* things about God through this dim and damaged reflection of him in our natural humanness, just as we can see some things reflected in a broken mirror. But there are other things about God which our own brokenness makes very confusing and hard to sort out (not to mention distasteful). Moreover, our status as creatures puts us in a very difficult situation if we wish to meet the Creator. Here's why:

Suppose Hamlet is looking around at his world. He would, as we have done, discover much to indicate that there was some sort of Mind behind his world — some Shakespeare out there — but there would also be a great deal to confuse and baffle him about the nature and purposes of that Mind. If he wanted to, he could, as we have done, try to get to know that Mind better by puzzling about the order of the world it has created. He could, as we have done, wonder about why there is evil in that world, and why certain things happen there. He could, as we have

---

[8] Pius XII, *Humani Generis*, 561.

done, guess from the fact that he is able to speak in beautiful poetry that the Mind that made him must have something of Beauty about it as well. He could, as we have done, discern even from the fact of evil in his world that there is a demand on him and everybody to be good and just. But there is one thing Hamlet could never do. He could never break out of his world and get into Shakespeare's world. If Hamlet is to talk to Shakespeare, Shakespeare will have to initiate the conversation.

Now we are to God as Hamlet is to Shakespeare. We are his creatures. We can make some good guesses about him based on what we see. We can infer that he exists. We can infer that he is an amazing artist. We can infer that he wants us to do the right thing (based on the fact that conscience seems to be built into us). But we also suffer with having our world and ourselves as distorted by sin as Hamlet's is. The mirror that should reflect Shakespeare clearly is broken and Hamlet cannot understand him all that well based simply on reason and looking at stuff around him. Moreover, Hamlet cannot, under any power of his own, leave his world to enter Shakespeare's. So if Hamlet is to know a lot more detail about Shakespeare — much less meet him — it is up to Shakespeare to make the first move and tell Hamlet about himself.

Scripture is the story of how God began to do just that in *our* world. It is the story of how God made a good world, how that world rebelled against him, and how he set about winning back a fallen humanity to participate in his divine nature after we threw it all away. This takes us to the next way in which God reveals himself: through the Sacred Tradition, both written and unwritten, of his people.

2

The Earliest Revelations of God

By natural reason man can know God with certainty, on the basis of his works. But there is another order of knowledge, which man cannot possibly arrive at by his own powers: the order of divine Revelation.

— Catechism of the Catholic Church, no. 50

To continue our metaphor from the previous chapter, the Catholic Church points us to Scripture as the means by which the divine Shakespeare shows us how he stepped into the world of all us Hamlets to show us wonders, teach us things, and call us to glories we could never have imagined on the basis of natural revelation alone. The first part of Scripture, the Old Testament or Hebrew Bible, chronicles the spiritual roots of the human race, the primordial disaster known as the Fall and then zeroes in on a particular people — the Jews — whom God chose for the strangest and most glorious mission in history. In this chapter, we will sketch the two most primeval revelations recorded in Scripture and begin to get our bearings a bit as we embark upon the story of that mission.

For many people, laying eyes on the Old Testament for

the first time is as puzzling as it was for me when I tried to read the Bible at age thirteen. We find ourselves in a *strange* world. Here is a creation story that sounds mythic. There is a tale of global flood. Here is God commanding Abraham to kill his own son in Genesis and forbidding child sacrifice in Isaiah. Here is a set of instructions, detailed down to the last particulars, about how to separate the fat from the internal organs of a freshly killed goat. There is a mysterious pillar of fire fending off the approach of the Egyptian army as it attempts to charge the fleeing Israelites. People are killed for gathering firewood on the wrong day and forgiven for committing murder and adultery. Some of the Old Testament appears to be wedding poetry, some of it poetic diatribes about 3,500-year-old Near-Eastern political intrigues, some of it enigmatic imagery of men wrestling with angels. It is chock full of smoking pots and firebrands passing between the severed halves of an animal carcass, prophets lying naked on their sides, bronze snakes hoisted up on poles, and various other things which, we feel sure, must be pregnant with some mysterious meaning. Once again, it's a little like playing *Myst* and we murmur, "If only we had a Key to what it's all about."

The good news is, we do (or rather God does). But just as I, as a father, have not given my children instant access to all the cheat sheets for *Myst* available on the Internet, so God, in his wisdom, chose not to give the human race his entire revelation at once but rather to prepare us so that when the Key was finally given, we would be ready.

So rather than jumping to the end of the story, let's begin, as God did . . .

In the Beginning

In discussing how revelation "unfolded over time" we are starting to speak of revelation as a kind of story. And as the King in *Alice in Wonderland* observed, a story must begin at the beginning, go on till we come to the end, then stop. But the very idea that revelation can *be* a story is not something that has been believed always and everywhere. In fact, for most of human history people did not believe in history as we understand it today. They believed that life was futile, that time was a circle and not a story line, and that the world was not so much going somewhere as going nowhere, like a sort of cosmic merry-go-round. In contrast to this was the peculiarly Jewish conception of history as having, just as the King says the good story should, a beginning, middle, and end.

That story, and that revelation beyond what we could know just by looking around, begins in the book of Genesis with three critical events: the Creation of the World, the Creation of Humankind and the Fall.

1. "God Created the Heavens and the Earth"

The first of these events is, of course, the Creation of the World. Much is made in these post-Darwinian days of the supposed "unscientific errors" of the creation account in Genesis 1. Contrarily, some fundamentalists wish to argue that Genesis is a perfectly scientific account. In short, the modern debate between fundamentalists and secularists centers on whether Genesis is good or bad science. What seldom enters into these crashing and chaotic debates is the still, small voice of Catholic teaching which reminds us that we should read every biblical text according to the original intention of the writer and not according to our own. If we take that counsel seriously and apply it to Genesis we suddenly discover something surprising. Namely, that the ancient Hebrew writer is not concerned to give a good *or* a bad scientific account. For he is not interested in *science* at all. It turns out we moderns (who are heirs to a Greco-Roman, Aristotelian, Christian, Enlightenment, and scientific worldview to which the author of Genesis was not privy) are beginning our reading of Genesis with an entirely different set of questions in our minds than were occupying the minds of ancient Jews.

Consider: when we moderns think of sun, moon, star, plant, reptile, insect, bird, and beast, we have been trained since we were knee-high to a grasshopper to think in terms of astronomy, physics, botany, or zoology. So we naturally assume that Genesis is trying to do early versions of these sciences to account for the creation it is contemplating. But, in fact, when the ancient Hebrew looked at the inventory of critters listed above, he did not see a scientific problem, he saw a spiritual one. For while Israel worshipped the one God (called Yahweh or Elohim in the Genesis narrative) every people surrounding Israel worshipped the critters listed in the creation account. That's a lot of peer pressure and Israel often succumbed to it.

Viewed from this perspective, we begin to realize that the question Genesis is primarily focusing on in the creation account revolves around "who" and "why" and not, as modern scientific questions do, around "how" "when" and "what." If you don't believe that, read the end of the book of Job (38–41), which is about the closest the ancient Hebrew mind gets to contemplating science questions about how the world was made. God's basic commentary about science questions there is: "I'm not interested in answering that question at the moment. We have more important matters to discuss. Let's talk about you and me, not the machinery by which I made stuff."

Seen in this light, the amazing thing about the Genesis account is how sane it is. Even though all the nations surrounding Israel are steeped in the idolatrous worship of practically every critter you can name in the inventory of created items from Genesis 1, and even though Israel is fiercely monotheistic, Genesis does not make the mistake of playing the either/or game ("Either God is good or creatures are good") and declaring creation an evil rival to God. Genesis does not lay out a story in which all material things are snares and deceptions calculated to lead us away from God. Instead, the inspired writer strikes just the right balance: these creatures are good, O Israel, but they are not God. Their goodness comes *from* the good God who made heaven and earth. And so God looks out on a creation which appears to offer endless competitors to his glory, and calls it good, rather than condemning it as a hotbed of idols. For he is the true author of all of its goodness and has, in the end, nothing to fear from it.

Nor, by the way, have we in this age of supposed "science vs. religion." For when we recognize the true intent of Genesis we begin to see that the so-called "quarrel between science and religion" is a quarrel between apples and oranges. If you start by asking different questions, you will arrive at different answers. If you start by asking "who" and "why" you will get different answers than when you ask "how," "when," and "what." But "different" does not mean "opposed."

2. *"Let Us Make Man in Our Image"*

This lack of a real quarrel becomes even clearer when we move past this prologue to the first main movements of the human drama beginning with the creation of Adam and Eve.

Once again, Scripture is addressing questions largely irrelevant to science and science (when it sticks to its proper subject) is treating issues largely irrelevant to the central points Genesis is trying to make about the origins and dignity of the human person. The Catholic Faith has always known this. That is why John Hardon, S.J. says in his *Catholic Catechism*,

> Before modern evolutionary theories were in vogue, the ancient Fathers and later Doctors of the Church, along with theologians, held that some special action of God was operative in the formation of the first man's body; this was distinct from the ordinary cooperation of the First Cause with the physical causes built into created nature. Only two main questions were raised prior to modern evolutionism: whether and to what extent God used above natural agencies, like angelic, in the formation of Adam's body; and whether the "dust from the soil" of Genesis implied a body divinely prepared beforehand to receive a rational soul before actual infusion, or whether the body was predisposed for receiving a spirit in the very act when God "breathed into his nostrils a breath of life and man became a living being." (Genesis 2:7)

But since the theories of evolution have been popularized, theologians have come to agree that transformism, or the evolution of the first man's body from a lower species, is compatible with the faith.[1]

Pope Pius XII said the same thing in his *Address to the Pontifical Academy of Sciences* (November 30, 1941), and in fact, bound the faithful to only three "elements [that] must be retained as certainly attested by the sacred author [of Genesis], without any possibility of an allegorical interpretation." These are:

1. The essential superiority of man in relation to other animals, by reason of his spiritual soul.

2. The derivation in some way of the first woman from the first man.

3. The impossibility that the immediate father or progenitor of man could have been other than a human being, that is, the impossibility that the first man could have been the son of an animal, generated by the latter in the proper sense of the term. In context, the statement reads, "Only from a man can another man descend, whom he can call father and progenitor."

This was borne out again in October 1996 when Pope John Paul II, standing in the context of a train of Catholic thought which stretched back to the Church Fathers said, in essence, "Looks like there's some good evidence

---

[1] John Hardon, S.J., *The Catholic Catechism* (Garden City: Doubleday, 1975), p. 93.

for some sort of biological evolution."[2] That is, he said, as so many Catholics have already said, that there is nothing in divine revelation that particularly forbids you to believe that God made Adam from the dust of the earth r-e-a-l-l-y s-l-o-w-l-y rather than instantaneously (and used other creatures to somehow assist in the process) so long as you bear in mind that God did, in fact, create man and woman (particularly the soul, which is made directly by God and is not a result of the collision of atoms). In the words of Hardon, "The Magisterium of the Church does not forbid that the theory of evolution concerning the origin of the human body as coming from pre-existent and living matter — for the Catholic faith obliges us to hold that human souls are immediately created by God — be investigated and discussed by experts as far as the present state of human science and sacred theology allow."[3]

This caveat about God's special providence in creating human beings is very important. For just as it is essential that students of Scripture not take Scripture as a science text, so it is also important for students of "the book of nature" (i.e., scientists) not to overstep their field and start pronouncing on areas in which science has no competence. Though it is not as common today, one can still hear people say foolish things like "Science has disproven the existence of God or the soul or the miraculous." Examples of this sort of overreach can be found in the work of Carl Sagan, for instance, who assures us (just as though he

---

[2] Pope John Paul II, *Message to the Pontifical Academy of Sciences* (October 22, 1996).
[3] Pius XII, *Humani Generis*: Denzinger 2327 (3896).

knows) that the physical universe "is all that is or ever was or ever will be."[4] In fact, Sagan can no more know this by peering through a telescope than by looking through a window. His claim is based, not on scientific evidence of any sort, but on a materialist philosophy which springs from his own psycho-emotional outlook. Likewise, popular author Richard Dawkins purports to tell us in books like *The Blind Watchmaker* that he knows for a fact that living things are not designed and that there is no Designer. But this is more a faith statement than Genesis is. For Dawkins cannot know this based on physical evidence either. He can only base his statement on a philosophy of materialism. Science can only measure physical things, it cannot measure spirit. It sees only nature, not supernature, just as a dog sees only black and white and not color. Asking science to comment on nonmaterial reality is like asking your dog to critique a painting by Van Gogh. A telescope does not acquire the power to look beyond nature simply because Sagan is peering through it. An electron microscope cannot disprove supernatural design merely because Dawkins wills it to do so. In short, science cannot even talk about anything that is not part of Nature. The Hubble Telescope can photograph things that are very far away, but no matter how hard it looks, it cannot photograph the face of God, for God is not part of this universe any more than an architect is part of the skyscraper he designs or a composer is a note on his sheet music. Science can show that certain fake miracles are fake (given enough evidence). It can only

---

[4] Carl Sagan, *Cosmos* (New York: Random House, 1980), p. 4.

say of real miracles, "We don't know if God caused it or why it happened."

This brings us back to what we have already seen: that the creation account is mainly interested in *who* and *why* not *what, when* or *how*. To the question of *who* Genesis gives two huge answers: God and us. God creates us. To the question of *why*, Genesis answers that he creates us not as toys or as servants to keep the universe ticking while he takes an extended break. Nor does he create us to kill us as flies for his entertainment (a very common conception of deity in neighboring Mesopotamia). Nor does he create us because he is lonely and needs someone to talk to. He does not create from *need* at all. He creates out of *bounty* and *love*.

He creates us "in his image and likeness" (Genesis 1:27). And curiously, his "image and likeness" is not Adam alone, but Adam-and-Eve together. This is why the text says: "So God created man in his own image, in the image of God he created him; *male and female* he created them" (Genesis 1:27).

3. "It is Not Good for Man to be Alone"

In fact, so insistent is God on the importance of man and woman together, that for the first time in the whole creation account, God looks at Adam alone in the Garden and says, "It is *not* good" (Genesis 1:18). Something essential is missing from the makeup of the creature that images God if that creature is alone. Adam without Eve is less than the image of God.

And so God does something charmingly childlike in the

story. He trots over critter after critter for Adam to inspect
as a possible "partner."

Dog? No.

Cat? No.

Porcupine? Uh, no thanks.

Giraffe? A little too tall and rather dimwitted.

Platypus? Not my type.

And so on through as many curious "partners" as you
might want to name. Is God really so stupid? asks the
modern mind. Is the author of Genesis such a savage as
to believe such silly things could have happened? But the
modern mind is again forgetting the way truth is being
communicated here. The instinct of the ancient Hebrew
mind, when it is trying to communicate an important truth,
is not to fling out an abstract philosophical dictum, but to
tell the truth via *story*. In the previous chapter, we discussed
the abstract statement, "Human beings are radically different from all other creatures" and noted that many modern
people tend to view this as human arrogance and pride.
In our culture, the claim "Humans are not like the rest
of nature" still meets with enormous resistance from those
whose minds are steeped in a vague evolutionism which
dictates that humans are just exceptionally clever pieces of
meat, different in degree, but not in kind from the rest
of the animal kingdom. The beauty of Genesis 2:18–25 is
that it immediately yanks us out of our vague philosophical
fog and brings us into vehement agreement with reality.
"What a stupid, primitive story!" we yell, "A porcupine
is not a suitable partner for Adam!" Yet we do not notice
that in yelling this, we are actually yelling, "No animal is
really the same sort of thing Adam is. He is human and
humans are radically different from beasts!" With a story

Scripture has gotten us to see in an instant what abstract philosophical argument has not gotten people to see in a century.

And so, getting back to the story, Adam is given Eve, made not from his foot so that he can step on her, nor from his head, so they can live in abstract philosophical contemplation together, but from his rib, nearest his heart. Finally the image of God is complete, neither Adam alone nor Eve alone, but Adam-and-Eve, unique among all creatures as the image of God. Marriage, wherein "the two shall become one flesh" (v. 2:24), is sacred, teaches Genesis.

But what is the creature who images God to do exactly? The biblical picture is threefold: servant kingship expressed in work, fruitfulness expressed in bringing forth other creatures in the image of God (Genesis 5:1), and worship. It is these three things, not "tool making" or being hairless bipeds, which mark us off from the rest of Creation. And these spring from the love of God and the love of one another.

Many people are surprised to hear that fruitfulness and work are God's ideas. They imagine that sex was what the Temptation in the Garden was all about and they are sure that work and childbirth were the curse. In reality, however, work, sex and fruitfulness are all given to Man and Woman as *blessings* before the serpent ever shows up.

> And God blessed them, and God said to them, "Be fruitful and multiply, and fill the earth and subdue it; and have dominion over the fish of the sea and over the birds of the air and over every living thing that moves upon the earth." (Genesis 1:28)
> The LORD God took the man and put him in the garden of Eden to till it and keep it. (Genesis 2:15)

God, it turns out, is not quite the killjoy we were led to believe. He seems to have conceived of both sex and work as fundamentally *good* things. Indeed, as Scott Hahn has pointed out, the Hebrew terms to describe "tilling and keeping" the Garden are only used in the Torah (the first five books of the Bible) to describe the duties of the Levitical priests in the Tabernacle (Numbers 3:7–8; 8:26; 18:5–6).[5] Work is *sacred*, just as life is sacred. We were made to be a royal line of priests.

So where did we get the idea that work and sex are supposed to somehow be bad?

4. *"You shall be like gods"*

Genesis 3 recounts the primordial catastrophe of our race. And once again, it is essential to know what the author is really trying to tell us here. Two mistakes are often made with this text. The first is to "take it literally" in the fundamentalist sense of saying, "God says there were talking snakes back then, so that is a Scientific Fact." The second mistake we can make is to say, "It's just a myth and therefore is 'true' in some vague and empty sense, but the Fall is not something that happened in history."

Both of these are misreadings of the text. It is not true that Scripture or the Catholic faith demands we believe in talking snakes. But neither is it true that Scripture and the Church do not demand we believe in a historical fall of Man. Scripture most emphatically does demand this and the Church has always taken the reality of a historical fall literally (Romans 5) just as it has always taken the reality

---

[5] Hahn, *A Father Who Keeps His Promises*, p. 54.

of Christ's historical crucifixion literally. But the *way* in which Genesis tells the story of this historical reality is not necessarily to be understood literally.

Think of it this way. In 2 Samuel 11, we read a historical record of a great crime committed by King David. He committed adultery with Bathsheba and then had her husband murdered to cover the crime. This is real history that really happened. Now read 2 Samuel 12:1–15. The prophet Nathan comes and "tells the story" of what David did in order to confront David with his crime. But instead of using newspaper language to tell the tale, he uses *figurative* language to describe a real event. Nathan tells David, "A rich man had a feast, but instead of killing one of his own sheep and serving it, he robbed a poor man of his only ewe and served that instead." When David condemns the "rich man", Nathan responds "*You* are the man!" and confronts David with his crime of adultery and murder. Is Nathan denying the historicity of David's crime by using figurative language to describe it? No, he is simply telling history in a very different way — a way perfectly clear to David.

Same here. Genesis tells us, in mythic language, of a historical disaster: the first humans rebelled against God. Under the mysterious influence of an evil angelic intelligence which later revelation will describe using the image of "the great dragon" and "that ancient serpent" and name "the devil and Satan" (Rev 12:9), we sought to "be like God, knowing good and evil" (Genesis 3:5). And in that hour, the union of our race with God was broken and we lost something we were meant to have.

In fact, Genesis tells the same story under different figures several times. The figures differ (Cain and Abel [Genesis 4:1–16], Lamech's boasting for killing [Genesis 4:23–24], the story of the Flood [Genesis 6–9], the cursing of Canaan [Genesis 9:18–27], and the Tower of Babel [Genesis 11]) but the point that is driven home is the same: There is something radically wrong with us, something that should not be wrong since we began in a state of grace and union with God but threw it away. We should be good, we should be happy, we should know God, but we aren't and we don't. Something in our remotest origins has been wrenched out of our makeup by the primordial sin of pride. We are fallen when we might not have been, had our First Parents not rejected the life God offered them (symbolized by the Tree of Life) and tried instead to be gods on their own. When they lost that something, they lost it for us, for they had nothing to pass on to us. And so we are born with a sort of spiritual birth defect — a thing missing from our souls where something *should* have been — that inevitably winds up making us repeat their sins of pride by trying to set up on our own apart from God (with the usual disastrous results played out in every newspaper from the *Babylonian Herald* to the *New York Times*).

It is because of this primordial haywiredness of our race rooted in the sin of our First Parents ("original sin" is the technical term for it) that work and fruitfulness now pain us.

> To the woman he said, "I will greatly multiply your pain in childbearing; in pain you shall bring forth children, yet your desire shall be for your husband, and he shall rule over you." And to Adam he said, "Because you have listened to the voice of your wife, and have eaten of the tree of which I commanded you, 'You shall not eat of it,' cursed is the ground because of you; in toil you shall eat of

it all the days of your life; thorns and thistles it shall bring forth to you; and you shall eat the plants of the field. In the sweat of your face you shall eat bread till you return to the ground, for out of it you were taken; you are dust, and to dust you shall return." (Genesis 3:16–19)

Marriage, fruitfulness, rule, work, worship — all these were given to us before the Fall and are good in themselves. But they, like we, are broken by the Fall. And so they are difficult and distorted, like trying to see the face of God through a shattered mirror. But worse than this, our very lives, after the Fall, come to frustration and finally, death. "You are dirt and to dirt you shall return" says God to his beloved Adam. And so it is.

But it is not the final word. God does two things before he exiles us from Paradise (seemingly forever). First, he makes a mysterious promise, not to Eve, but to the serpent:

"I will put enmity between you and the woman, and between your seed and her seed; he shall bruise your head, and you shall bruise his heel." (Genesis 3:15)

So our fruitfulness, though damaged, is not destroyed. The race shall continue, though subject to futility and death. And the "seed of the woman" will somehow be involved in "bruising" the serpent's head.

Second, God clothes us. And he clothes us, not with fig leaves, but with the *skins of animals* (Genesis 3:21). Our nakedness, discovered to our shame in the moment of the Fall (v. 7) is covered by bloody death. What the significance of that gesture is, we are not told. But it is hard to contemplate it long without sensing there is some very great significance to it indeed.

And so, "hand in hand, with wand'ring steps and slow"[6]
Adam and Eve depart into exile from Eden. The very first
bit of biblical revelation is now complete. We know that
Creation is good and God is its (and our) Maker. We know
man and woman are in the image and likeness of God in a
way that sets them off from all other creatures. We know
that marriage is sacred. We know we were made to work
as kings and queens, worship as priests and be fruitful as
fathers and mothers to the glory of God. We know we fell
and made those three tasks much harder. And we know
that, despite the curse of pain and even death, God did not
abandon us. Apparently, he had further plans.

Noah

The next major figure in Genesis is Noah. Much is made
of arguments about the historicity of Noah's flood and we
will not re-examine here the question of the exact historical
details of the Flood narrative any more than of the Creation narrative since the writer himself is not interested in
giving us exact scientific history but divine truth. Therefore, what we will look at, as with the account of Adam
and Eve, is the *way* in which Genesis uses the story of the
Great Flood (a common theme in Mesopotamian literature
and indeed in many world literatures) in order to relate
truth about God's relationship with the human race.

The story is, of course, so familiar that we may not really be listening to it any more what with the hundreds of
retellings in every *Golden Book of Favorite Bible Stories for
Children*. We think it's a "charming" story, a story that has

---

[6] John Milton, *Paradise Lost*, 12.

been milked of all its significance for adults long ago. But we forget that it was not written for children any more than the story of the murder of Abel was penned for the entertainment of the Tinker Toy set. It is a narrative of very serious purpose aimed at grownups (albeit grownups with teachable hearts like those of children). Let's look at it afresh and consider what the writer of Genesis has in mind.

In the story of Adam and Eve we see God's covenant with man given through marriage. In the story of Noah, we see that covenant expand from a couple to a family. Not just Noah and his wife are saved from the Flood; their sons and daughters-in-law are as well. The circle of blessing has expanded.

But it is still a very small circle in the narrative. And this is so, not because God does not wish to bless but because man, recapitulating the rejection of God in the Garden, does not wish to be blessed. And so, "The LORD saw that the wickedness of man was great in the earth, and that every imagination of the thoughts of his heart was only evil continually. And the LORD was sorry that he had made man on the earth, and it grieved him to his heart. So the LORD said, 'I will blot out man whom I have created from the face of the ground, man and beast and creeping things and birds of the air, for I am sorry that I have made them'" (Genesis 6:5–7).

Other Mesopotamian tellings of this sort of story give a very different, almost burlesque, cast to the tale. For instance, an ancient Sumerian flood myth called the *Epic of Atrahasis*[7] explains the Flood this way:

---

[7] The Atrahasis Epic can be found in a variety of translations such as *Ancient Near Eastern Texts Relating to the Old Testament, Third Edi-*

600 years, less than 600, passed,
And the country was as noisy as a bellowing bull.
The god grew restless at their racket,
Enlil had to listen to their noise.
He addressed the great gods,
"The noise of mankind has become too much,
I am losing sleep over their racket."

Enlil is not exactly the most awe-inspiring god in ancient literature, yet neither is he alone. Often in ancient accounts, the deities are petty twerps who happen to command Phenomenal Cosmic Powers. In contrast, Genesis holds fast to the basic theme that the reason for the judgement of the Flood upon the earth is because of human wickedness. Once again, the basic theme is of a stroke of justice (not mere irritation over noisy downstairs neighbors) dealt by an outraged Heaven against a grossly sinful humanity which has very deliberately rejected life and love.

Beyond this, what is fascinating is the way in which the story of Noah recapitulates the first story of the Creation and Fall. As Scott Hahn points out:

> Interestingly, the description of God's flood-judgment is notably similar to the pattern of divine Creation in the opening chapters of Genesis. In both cases, a new world would emerge from the chaotic waters of "the deep" (see Genesis 1:2; 7:11). The number "seven" also stands out prominently in both accounts. As the sign of God's "rest" at creation, it is closely linked to Noah (whose name means "rest" or "relief," see Genesis 5:29). Likewise, Noah was ordered to take seven pairs of clean animals into the ark (see Genesis 7:2), which he did, before closing the door: "After seven days the waters of the flood came upon the

---

tion with Supplement, James B. Pritchard, editor (Princeton: Princeton University Press, 1969).

earth" (Genesis 7:10). And in the seventh month, the ark came to "rest" upon Mount Ararat (see Genesis 8:4). After a long wait, Noah sent out a dove every seven days (see Genesis 8:10–12), until his family was finally able to disembark.

After disembarking, Adam's divine commission was repeated for Noah: "be fruitful and multiply, and fill the earth" (Genesis 9:1). God also restored Noah to Adam's former position of dominion over the beasts (see Genesis 9:2). Finally, the Father renewed the Creation covenant with Noah (see Genesis 9:9), revealing to him the sign of the new covenant: "I set my bow in the cloud, and it shall be a sign of the covenant between me and the earth" (Genesis 9:13).

Clearly the flood account is presented as the re-creation event. And not only the flood but perhaps also the Fall, in view of other parallels between Adam and Noah: both find themselves in garden or vineyard (see Genesis 2:15; 9:20), where they consume a fruit that exposes their sin and nakedness (see Genesis 3:6–7; 9:21) and elicits a curse (see Genesis 3:14–19; 9:25), which redounds to future progeny (Cain and Canaan).[8]

Several things begin to emerge when we see the connection between the covenant with Adam and the covenant with Noah. The first is this: it, like the covenant with Adam, is not a "Jewish" covenant but a covenant with the entire human race. This means that the wording of this covenant is important for us Gentiles to pay attention to for it is one of those rare instances in the Old Testament when God is speaking to us directly. And when we listen, we notice something — something so obvious that we take it for granted. And yet it is something which was not at

---

[8] Hahn, *A Father Who Keeps His Promises*, pp. 84–85.

all taken for granted by people, even highly educated people, before the Judeo-Christian revelation made it a settled assumption on the part of Western culture.

That something is the truth of the unity of the human family. Genesis, in hammering home the stories of Adam and Eve and again of Noah, insists that God "made from one every nation of men to live on all the face of the earth, having determined allotted periods and the boundaries of their habitation" (Acts 17:26). In America, with our deeply ingrained democratic culture, we have lived so long with the settled and certain assumption that "all men are created equal" that it is very difficult for us to imagine thinking in any other way. The very fact that even racists in our culture are embarrassed by their racism and must find some way to hide it or explain it away shows how settled this assumption of equality is.

But in antiquity there was nothing *less* obvious than the idea of human unity or equality. Aristotle, one of the most educated people of the ancient world, was not at all embarrassed when he said that certain people were "natural slaves" and wrote concerning them, "Now instruments are of various sorts; some are living, others lifeless . . . Thus, too, a possession is an instrument for maintaining life. And so, in the arrangement of the family, a slave is a living possession, and property a number of such instruments; and a servant is himself an instrument for instruments."[9] In short, for him a slave was something like a talking plow and he was not embarrassed to say so because his education had never included the biblical teaching about human equality. He did not live in a culture, as we do, that had had this bib-

---

[9] Aristotle, *Politics* I, 5, (1253.4; 1254a17–1254b40).

lical teaching kneaded into it for two millennia. Likewise, Tacitus, another highly educated ancient unaware of biblical revelation, speaks with cold contempt of practically everybody outside his class.[10] This mutual antagonism which has plagued humanity since the Fall has often manifested itself by some small tribe or other declaring itself "the human beings" and assigning all other members of the human race to some degraded status. And it plagues us to this day with the curse of racism and the insane theories of the "Master Race" that ignited the Holocaust.

The Noah account, in contrast, sharply undercuts all this. It emphatically affirms the reality that, however fractious and even evil the human family can be, it cannot be divided into a master race and various "subhuman" classes. We are all, even slaves, sons and daughters of Adam and Noah. There are no lesser breeds.

The next thing the story of Noah does is implement the first and most obvious remedy to the problem of evil. It is the remedy that occurred to the three-year-old daughter of a friend of mine who, upon hearing the story of Adolf Hitler for the first time, declared, "If I had been alive back then, I would have told Hitler to be good." When her father informed her that Hitler would have been bad anyway, she responded, "Then I would've poked his eyes out and cut his head off."

Now, truth to tell, this little girl's solution is the one we all, in our heart of hearts, feel certain would work when we contemplate some heinous crime that we read about in the newspapers. Just kill the bad guys and let decent,

---

[10] Tacitus, *The Annals of Imperial Rome* (New York: Viking Penguin, 1971).

taxpaying "ordinary" people go on about their lives. That should do the trick. It is a prayer we find even in Scripture, such as when the psalmist prays in Psalm 139:19, "O that thou wouldst slay the wicked, O God, and that men of blood would depart from me, men who maliciously defy thee, who lift themselves up against thee for evil!"[11] So in the very childhood of the world, God grants this childish prayer. And as a result, one single solitary family escapes judgment on the Bad Guys while the whole world is annihilated. This should give us pause when we dally with such prayers in the future.

What should give us further pause is that even this radically simple solution to the problem of evil does not do the trick. As Hahn notes above, not only the Creation is recapitulated in the story of Noah, but the Fall as well. For Noah and his family suffer the effects of original sin just like the rest of us. As God himself observes, "The imagination of man's heart is evil from his youth" (Genesis 8:21). And so, practically before the last hoof has stepped out of the ark Noah is drunk and his son, Ham, has committed a sin so grave that once again a curse is invoked. The most obvious "solution" to the problem of evil turns out to not solve anything and brings the attentive reader of Genesis to the same fact confronted by Alexander Solzhenitsyn when he wrote, "If only there were evil people somewhere insidiously committing evil deeds and it were necessary only to separate them from the rest of us and destroy them. But the line dividing good and evil cuts through the heart of

---

[11] "As if it were surprising that such a simple remedy for human ills had not occurred to the Almighty." (C. S. Lewis, *Reflections on the Psalms* [New York: Harcourt, Brace & World, Inc., 1958]), p. 21.

every human being. And who is willing to destroy a piece of his own heart?"[12]

But that does not mean nothing has changed. The covenant with Noah recapitulates the covenant with Adam, but also ups the ante. God, having shown the futility of the "simple" solution to the problem of evil, promises to never again destroy the world by water (Genesis 9:8–17), which means that the "simple" solution to the problem of evil will no longer be open in the future. Further, God permits the imposition of the death penalty (Genesis 9:5–7) as a sign, paradoxically, of the sanctity of human life.[13] And in a mysterious clause, God permits the killing of animals (Genesis 9:3) with this strange caveat: "you shall not eat flesh with its life, that is, its blood." (Genesis 9:4). That clause, as we shall see, is pregnant with enormous significance, and (as we shall also see) with a significance which even its human author could not have anticipated.

---

[12] Alexander Solzhenitsyn, *The Gulag Archipelago, 1918–1956; An Experiment in Literary Investigation* (New York: Harper & Row, 1974–1978) Vol. 2, p. 615.

[13] Many people read this clause as "divine approval" for the death penalty. The difficulty with this is that God has previously refrained from visiting the death penalty on the murderers Cain and Lamech (Genesis 4:8–16; 23–24). In light of this, the text can just as easily be read as a *concession* to the reality of human evil, just as the texts permitting divorce are concessions, not expressions of divine approval, for divorce (Matthew 19:8). It is arguable that the primary teaching here is the sanctity of human life and that, though God *permits* capital punishment as he permitted divorce under the Mosaic Law, we can nonetheless say "from the beginning it was not so." This argument becomes all the stronger when we consider that the far graver sin of shedding the blood of God Incarnate brought, not capital punishment, but the prayer of forgiveness from the Divine Victim himself.

And so, from the family of Noah, as from Adam and
Eve, the human race is bidden to once again "be fruitful
and multiply" and spread out across the face of the earth
that, in the words of St. Paul, "they should seek God, in
the hope that they might feel after him and find him" (Acts
17:27). The stage is set for another and more mysterious
revelation of God, given not to Man, but to a man.

3

The Further Revelations of God

[God] selected one particular people and spent several centuries hammering into their heads the sort of God He was — that there was only one of Him and He cared about right conduct. Those people were the Jews, and the Old Testament gives an account of the hammering process.

— C. S. Lewis

Abraham

The third great moment in revelation involves yet another paradox. For while the first two covenants are made with the human race as a whole through Adam and Noah, the covenant with Abraham (at first known as "Abram") zeroes our attention in on one man to the apparent exclusion of the rest of the race. In that sense, the scope of the covenant seems to be much narrower. But in another sense, it is wider than ever. For the first covenant was with Adam and Eve (a married couple), and the second covenant was with Noah and his immediate kin (a household). But this third covenant is with the chieftain of a tribe.

At the mention of the word "tribe" the modern mind re-
coils. We moderns can cope with the idea of God's first two
covenants because they are at least made with the whole
human race. But when we get to Abram we start mutter-
ing, "God could have spared us a lot of trouble by casting
his net more widely, emphasizing more universality rather
than tribalism."

This thought comes as naturally as rain in spring to
minds conditioned to think in democratic terms as ours
are. Just as it was natural for ancients who lived almost
universally under monarchy to conceive of God as King,
so it is equally natural for moderns to force the universe
into a grid of uncompromising egalitarianism. We rankle
at the thought that God "elects" people like Abram.

And yet Scripture points us to an amazing paradox.
Namely, that in choosing the tribal chieftain Abram, God
was building the only real basis for universality in the
world.

Not that it looks that way at first, of course. God's first
promise to Abram confirms the worst modern fears of
what the Old Testament is supposedly all about: "I will
make of you a great nation, and I will bless you, and make
your name great" (Genesis 12:2). Here, we fancy, is just
the sort of ancient Israelite chest-thumping we expected
we would find. It seems to be just the sort of "God is on
our side" rhetoric we might expect to prop up an ideology
of conquest by an ancient tribal people. But when we look
closer, we shall see that there is a curious third clause to the
promise made to Abram. It is this: "I will bless those who
bless you, and him who curses you I will curse; and *by you
all the families of the earth shall bless themselves*" (Genesis
12:3). What that clause means in its fullness we shall take

up later in this book, but what we can immediately note is that, whatever else is the case, this passage means that God has not forgotten the rest of the world while he attends to Abram. So let us trust God enough at present to follow him as he (apparently) narrows his attention from Humanity to this one solitary man. And as we do so, let us contemplate the reality that we moderns, who are used to thinking of "universality" as statisticians do, have difficulty here because we think of "Humanity" while God thinks of persons. This difference between divine and human ways of approaching things shows up a very important fact: namely, real revelation can only proceed in a personal way, through human persons, not through mass advertising. And so God begins the drama of redemption from the Fall, not with a series of TV ads aimed at appealing to millions, but with the friendship of one man. He elects one human person — Abram — and begins the process of revealing himself, one person at a time, first to a tribe, then, as he promised, to a nation, then to a kingdom, and, in the fullness of time, to the world.

Naturally such elections are painful, especially for the Elect. People grow fond of their roots. We love our fathers and mothers and all they worked so hard and well to build. Nobody appreciated that more than Abram, who is commanded by God to "Go from your country and your kindred and your father's house to the land that I will show you" (Genesis 12:1). This is not, as we might think from watching certain movies, as though a lone mystic were to be struck by religious enthusiasm and head for the hills by himself. Abram, as a tribal chieftain, has responsibility for a considerable crowd of people. It is a huge, daunting, and seemingly bizarre logistical problem for a man of Abram's stature and status to pull up stakes from the comfortable existence he has enjoyed in Haran (in modern-day Iraq) and wander off into the blue. To get the hang of it, imagine the president of a medium-sized company telling his family, his more remote relatives, and all 200 of his employees, "God wants us to depart by rocket for another planet. We will be leaving next week. I don't know which planet it is but God will let me know when we get there." That's faith.

"And I will make of you a great nation"

This is the first part of the three-part promise to Abram. And though God follows through on it, as the story of Abram and the rest of the Old Testament shows, our Lord does so on his own timetable. So the gulf in time between the promise of a son and the fulfillment is over twenty years — twenty years of testing and refining. Abram and Sarai, however, don't know they are being refined. They simply think they are getting older and older, a fact that weighs on both their minds a great deal.

Abram begins his time of testing by sojourning in Canaan (and later in Egypt). But, like all saints-in-training, he does not always succeed in being saintly. Specifically, he wimps out at the thought that Pharaoh might be interested in his wife, Sarai, and so tells a half-truth: he says Sarai is his sister (she's his half-sister actually), but neglects to mention her marital status, so that Pharaoh takes her home with him for a while (Genesis 12:10–20). God intervenes to prevent Abram from facilitating adultery and gently sees to it that his wife is restored to him with her chastity intact. Evidently Abram is less than confident at the outset that the fulfillment of God's promise of a mighty nation springing from his offspring is going to involve Sarai's participation.

But though Abram wavers, he does not fail in his faith. Indeed, despite his slip here, he continues to be faithful both to God and to his kin. His nephew Lot gripes to him that the land of Canaan (that is, present-day Israel) ain't big enough for the both of them what with their servants, flocks, herds and such. So Abram graciously offers Lot first pick of the best land (Genesis 13). Lot promptly indulges his selfish little heart, snaps up Abram's offer in a heartbeat, and heads off to a little town called Sodom. This town, which will face more dramatic difficulties later, is one of several communities all sending soldiers out to beat each other up for the glory of their respective Fatherlands. In one such campaign, Sodom's team loses the battle and the winning army overruns both Sodom and Lot's piece of real estate. Lot and his family are taken prisoner.

And so, Abram, good kinsman that he is, goes to rescue his ingrate nephew and family (Genesis 14). He succeeds and, on the way home, is met by a very mysterious figure named Melchizedek, "king of Salem" and "priest of God Most High" who (as far as the narrative is concerned) simply pops out of nowhere, blesses Abram with bread and wine, and receives a tenth of all Abram had. He then vanishes from the narrative without a trace, leaving us to sense Something Important Just Happened. And this impression is doubled because when another potentate — the king of Sodom — also tries to bless Abram with some of the spoil from the battle, Abram will have none of it. Clearly, Melchizedek is a significant person, but just what his significance is goes unexplained — at least for the moment.

The next scene (Genesis 15) reveals a reiteration of the promise made to Abram (and of Abram's faith and doubt). God declares once again that Abram will become a great nation. Abram declares once again his guess that such a promise, however it is fulfilled, will not happen through Sarai:

> "O Lord GOD, what wilt thou give me, for I continue childless, and the heir of my house is Eliezer of Damascus?" And Abram said, "Behold, thou hast given me no offspring; and a slave born in my house will be my heir." (Genesis 15:2–3)

Abram trusts God to fulfil his word somehow, but assumes that this will be done in some mundane way, like making his head servant, Eliezer, the heir to his fortune. God, however, has other, considerably bigger, plans.

> And behold, the word of the LORD came to him, "This man shall not be your heir; your own son shall be your heir." And he brought him outside and said, "Look toward heaven, and number the stars, if you are able to number them." Then he said to him, "So shall your descendants be." (Genesis 15:4–5)

And here is the impressive thing about Abram. Perhaps it was the habit of obedience he had already begun to cultivate by going to Canaan when God spoke. Perhaps it was the softness of heart he opened himself to by being so gentle with his selfish nephew. Maybe it was a healthy self-doubt caused by seeing how he had wimped out in giving Sarai to Pharaoh. Or maybe it was all three and a good dollop of the grace of God besides. But at any rate, Scripture records something amazing about Abram's response to this improbable promise, something that characterized Abram's whole life:

And he believed the LORD; and he reckoned it to him as
righteousness. (Genesis 15:6)

God, for his part, does something which characterizes
his dealings with human beings throughout the Old Testament: he stoops down to their level, in this case by en-
gaging in a ritual which seems bizarre to us but which
made perfect sense to the original readers of Genesis. He
bids Abram kill several animals in sacrifice, arrange the
halves of their carcasses opposite one another, and then,
in a strange vision, passes between the halves under the
symbol of a "smoking fire pot and a flaming torch" (Genesis 15:17). This rite, known as "cutting a covenant" was
an accepted practice in Near Eastern culture at the time,
by which the two parties swore an oath and invoked a
curse upon themselves that what happened to the animals
might happen to the person who broke the oath. God, in
the childhood of the world, sees fit to bend down and re-
assure us children with a "cross my heart and hope to die"
in order to strengthen our small faith. And Abram will
need such strength, for though he believes God will give
him children, he still is not sold on the idea that it could
possibly involve Sarai.

Which is, perhaps, why he listens so readily to Sarai's
bright idea that he bed her maidservant Hagar so that she
can "obtain children by her" (Genesis 16:2). This, to be
fair to Abram and Sarai, was also an accepted practice in
the ancient Near East, but it was still not what God had
in mind. Nonetheless, God is patient with Abram's impa-
tience and, in time, makes Hagar's son, Ishmael, a great
nation too (though not the chosen one, as we shall see)
(Genesis 16:10–12).

What God *did* have in mind is not shown to Abram for another fourteen years. Genesis 17 tells us when Abram is 99 years old and Sarai trailing not far behind, God chooses that moment — twenty-five years after promising Abram a son — to do two things. First, he once again swears an oath to Abram that "I will make my covenant between me and you, and will multiply you exceedingly" (Genesis 17:2). God then re-names Abram "Abraham" (which means "father of a multitude"), and commands "Every male among you shall be circumcised. You shall be circumcised in the flesh of your foreskins, and it shall be a sign of the covenant between me and you" (Genesis 17:10–11). Then he drops a bombshell on Abraham.

God announces the promise of an heir will now *really* be fulfilled. And not through Eliezer, nor through Hagar, but through the last, most unlikely person in the world: Sarai (whom God re-named "Sarah"). So insistent is God on this point that he says it to Abraham twice: once in a personal apparition (Genesis 17:1) and again through three angelic messengers shortly thereafter (Genesis 18). Sarah's response to the news? The old lady cracks up laughing (Genesis 18:12). And she and Abraham laughed all the harder with joy when, a year later, their bouncing baby boy, Isaac (whose name means "laughter"), arrived on schedule. Here at long last is the one through whom God promises "I will establish my covenant" (Genesis 17:21).

But not before one final and harrowing trial. Abraham has already endured the loss of home. He then endures the loss of Ishmael, for Sarah demanded that he and Hagar be sent away once Isaac was born (Genesis 21:8–21). (Abraham acquiesces to this under God's assurance that the boy and Hagar will be cared for.) But these losses, painful as they were, are nothing compared to what God requires of him a few years later when, out of the blue, God calls him and says:

> "Take your son, your only son Isaac, whom you love, and go to the land of Moriah, and offer him there as a burnt offering upon one of the mountains of which I shall tell you." (Genesis 22:2)

Surely the words "only son" must have had a special bitterness for Abraham now that Ishmael was banished. All his hopes in God had been narrowed down to this one lad, Isaac. As all parents have felt in looking at their own children, everything Abraham loved and hoped for was summed up in the boy's face. And now, at the climax of his life, it appeared that God had set the whole thing up as some sort of exercise in cosmic sadism — a huge, ugly practical joke.

And yet, such was Abraham's faith that he obeyed anyway. God had never lied to him and so, however horribly things seemed to be going, Abraham doggedly went on trusting what God had told him about his covenant with Isaac, and trudged off as he commanded. We can only imagine the agony of confusion that must have gone through Abraham's mind as the old man and his boy toiled up the mountain carrying firewood and a torch. We can only guess at the stabbing anguish he must have felt when Isaac (perhaps with mounting tension and suspicion) asked, "Behold, the fire and the wood; but where is the lamb for a burnt offering?" (Genesis 22:7). And we can barely guess at the resolve of faith (tinged with bitter irony) Abraham must have felt when he resolutely replied, "God will provide himself the lamb for a burnt offering, my son" (Genesis 22:8).

It is also worth noting that Isaac showed his own faith in this hour. For the boy did not fight as he could easily have done. He trusted Abraham as Abraham trusted God. And so Isaac was bound, laid upon the wood, and Abraham lifted the knife to strike . . .

> But the angel of the LORD called to him from heaven, and said, "Abraham, Abraham!" And he said, "Here am I." He said, "Do not lay your hand on the lad or do anything to him; for now I know that you fear God, seeing you have not withheld your son, your only son, from me." And Abraham lifted up his eyes and looked, and behold, behind him was a ram, caught in a thicket by his horns; and Abraham went and took the ram, and offered it up as a burnt offering instead of his son. So Abraham called the name of that place The LORD will provide; as it is said to this day, "On the mount of the LORD it shall be provided." (Genesis 22:11–14)

Abraham had passed the supreme test. He loved God with all his heart, soul, mind and strength, holding back nothing. And so, God ratifies the last part of the promise given to him, that all the nations of the earth shall be blessed through him.

> "By myself I have sworn, says the LORD, because you have done this, and have not withheld your son, your only son, I will indeed bless you, and I will multiply your descendants as the stars of heaven and as the sand which is on the seashore. And your descendants shall possess the gate of their enemies, and by your descendants shall all the nations of the earth bless themselves, because you have obeyed my voice." (Genesis 22:16–18)

All the rest of Scripture will, in one way or another, be the story of the fulfillment of this tripartite promise to

Abraham of nationhood, kingdom, and worldwide blessing. What we initially imagined was just ancient barbaric
boasting shall turn out to portray Abraham as the waist of
some mystical hourglass through which the blessing of God
is to pour in ever-widening bounty to the whole world.

But, as is God's custom, it poured in his time, not ours.
And so, by measured pace, Scripture will show the covenant
with Abraham widen, next to Isaac, then to Jacob, then to
the twelve tribes of Israel who descend from Jacob's twelve
sons. And then, just when it seems obvious that they will
go on prospering forever as their rich great-grandfather
had done, the next great trial begins.

Israel, through the good offices of Jacob's son, Joseph,
goes down to Egypt during a time of famine. Joseph (in
a beautiful story we shall not retell here [Genesis 37–50])
had become Pharaoh's Right-Hand Man. And things were
pretty good while he was alive. But in the generations after
his death, the fortunes of the Israelites declined severely until "there arose a new king over Egypt, who did not know
Joseph" (Exodus 1:8) and Israel ended up, not a nation of
land barons, but a nation of slaves.

And so we arrive at the book of Exodus and the next
great moment in salvation history: the covenant with Moses.

Moses

Many of us, when we think of Moses the Lawgiver, naturally think of somebody with a rich, stentorian voice and
a square jaw framed with a flowing, dignified beard. We
think of a man rooted like an oak in deep wellsprings
of spirituality, a man confident of word and deed, a man
given to enunciating resonant phrases upon which to build

Western civilization. We think, in short, of Charlton Heston.

However, the man whom Mr. Heston played in Cecil B. DeMille's epic *The Ten Commandments* did not see himself this way. He saw himself as a sinner, as tongue-tied, as stuck in an agonizingly frustrating role and (many times) he saw himself as a failure — a self-estimate apparently confirmed when he died on the verge of achieving his life's work: taking possession of the "land flowing with milk and honey", the Holy Land. He once killed a man, he struggled with doubt, he was tempted to workaholism, he was hagridden by responsibility for a nation that continually treated him with contempt . . . and he is one of the greatest men who ever lived. Who was this Moses?

Moses was born during a time of bitter persecution for Israel. In his infancy, Exodus tells us, he was floated down the Nile in a basket to save him from the death sentence imposed by Egypt on all Hebrew male children. Found by Pharaoh's daughter and raised in the house of Pharaoh, Moses "was educated in all the wisdom of the Egyptians and was powerful in his words and deeds" (Acts 7:22). But when he was forty, something happened. He killed an Egyptian who was mistreating a fellow Hebrew and, in a foretaste of the gratitude he would typically receive for all well-meaning efforts on behalf of his people, he was promptly threatened with exposure to Pharaoh by a jealous countryman (Exodus 2:14).

So he flees Egypt one step ahead of the law and settles in Midian (on the east side of the Sinai peninsula with a nice big desert between him and Pharaoh). There he marries and there he has his first encounter with the Living God: the apparition at the Burning Bush (Exodus 3).

There God — "the God of Abraham, Isaac, and Jacob" as he calls himself in order to remind Moses of the covenant with Abraham — calls Moses to return to Egypt and lead Israel out of bondage to the Promised Land. Moses replies: "Pharaoh's not going to let you get away with this." God's answer: "I'll take care of Pharaoh." Moses doubts: "Why should anybody believe me?" God says, "I'll perform some miracles that will convince them." Moses hedges: "Could somebody else do the talking? I'm not good with words." God's final concession: "Your brother Aaron can do the talking. Now go!"

So Moses, still presumably unsure of himself, goes and confronts Pharaoh. Result: Pharaoh is so annoyed he doubles the workload of the Hebrew slaves and the Hebrews blame Moses (Exodus 5). Moses returns to Pharaoh and repeats the demand, "Let my people go" and this time backs it up with the first of ten plagues divinely visited on Egypt (Exodus 7–11). Finally, after the death of the first-born of Egypt, Pharaoh capitulates and lets Israel go, but not before second thoughts send Pharaoh after Israel one last time. He catches the runaway slaves on the shore of Yam Suph (the Sea of Reeds) and is about to finish them off when God performs the most unforgettable miracle in all of Jewish sacred history: he parts the sea and allows Israel to walk across before closing the waters over the heads of Pharaoh's pursuing troops (Exodus 14). It is this miraculous deliverance which is celebrated every year in the Passover seder — a deliverance and a meal which, as we shall see, was also pregnant with a significance of which its original participants could not have dreamed.

Israel is now free in body. But they are still slaves to Egypt in heart. And so begins the forty year period of the great wandering in the Sinai wilderness, where God slowly transforms this rabble of slaves into a *people*. It is period of prolonged frustration and anguish for Moses, with Israel continually thanking him for their rescue by complaining and wishing they could return to the fleshpots and bread of Egypt (Exodus 16:3), by grumbling against him (Exodus 17:2), and by organizing open rebellions against him (Numbers 16). Sometimes, Moses forgets that he can't carry this weight alone and forgets to delegate work to anybody else (until his father-in-law, Jethro, suggests it) (Exodus 18:14–26). Sometimes, Moses gives every indication that he is just as frustrated with God as with Israel, complaining aloud to the Almighty, "What shall I do with this people? A little more and they will stone me!" (Exodus 17:4).

But in addition to the aggravation, Moses receives stunning and unprecedented revelations from God. Most importantly, he receives the revelation of the covenant with Israel (Exodus 20).

The essence of the covenant with Moses was, like the covenant with Abraham, threefold. It involved creed, code, and cult. A creed says, "Here is what we must believe." A code says, "Here is what we must do." And a cult says, "Here is how we must worship." (The modern narrowing of the word "cult" to mean simply and solely "creepy and esoteric religion" is of very recent vintage, dating back to about the time of the Jim Jones murder/suicides in the late 1970s. "Cult" actually refers to any form of worship, legitimate or illegitimate.)

The creed of Israel is apparently simple and direct: "I am the LORD your God, who brought you out of the land of Egypt, out of the house of bondage" (Exodus 20:2). This is who God reveals himself to be. Also apparently simple and direct is the code given to Israel: the Ten Commandments and the various other laws for regulating everyday life in ancient Israel. Another way of putting both creed and code in a single sentence is found in Deuteronomy 6:4–5: "Hear, O Israel: The LORD our God is one LORD; and you shall love the LORD your God with all your heart, and with all your soul, and with all your might." And the cultic worship of Israel, for all its elaborate instructions and details (described, for instance, in the book of Leviticus) has at its root a simple insight: love *costs*.

And so, the covenant is sealed with the blood of sacrifice and a detailed sacrificial system — once again pregnant with a mysterious significance dating back to Noah — is inaugurated. Israel is provided with a sort of movable sanctuary tent called the Tabernacle and given extremely detailed instructions on every item of furniture in it including, in particular, the famous Ark of the Covenant (a reasonable facsimile of which was featured in the film *Raiders of the Lost Ark*). The Ark — a gold-overlaid wooden box containing the tablets of the law and topped by statuettes of two cherubim bowing to empty air — symbolized the Presence of the invisible God in a unique way. It was here, before the Holy One who "sits enthroned upon the cherubim" (Psalm 99:1) that the creed, code and cult of the God of Israel was focused. Had Israel only been given the creed, they might have become an association of professional theologians. Had they received only the code, they might have formed a society of ethicists. But instead, God called them to be "a kingdom of priests and a holy nation" (Exodus 19:6) and so he gave to Israel a whole way of life, teaching, *and* worship. Once again, it was all so apparently simple and direct.

Not so simple and direct, however, is the reality which is pounded home on the heels of this revelation and which will constitute the central problem of the Old Testament from that day forward. Namely, the reality that neither creed, code nor cult are really going to be kept in Israel.

Scripture emphasizes the direness of this problem in a dramatic way. For while Moses was on the mountain of God receiving these overwhelming revelations, Israel was in the meantime busy enlisting the aid of Moses' brother Aaron (of all people) to fashion a Golden Calf (Exodus 32) which they proceeded to worship, saying "This is your God, O Israel, who brought you out of the land of Egypt." Moses does not even have time to get down off the mountain before Israel, fresh from some of the most spectacular displays of God's gracious power in history, manages to demonstrate its gratitude by worshipping a cow and indulging in orgies. Moses chastises them, to be sure, shattering the tablets of the law on the ground in symbolism of the way Israel had shattered the law in their hearts. But the most impressive thing about Moses in this moment is what he does *not* do: he does not reject Israel but intercedes for them, crying out to God to spare them when the Lord threatens to exterminate them on the spot. In this, we see Moses, all unaware (as Abraham was), being fashioned by God's hand into a saint, willing to risk death in order that his sinful people might live. And God, of course, grants his prayer.

This little vignette more or less summarizes the whole of the rest of the drama of the Old Testament. God extends grace. Israel drops the ball. God permits judgment to come. Israel repents (to some degree or other). God forgives and, slow but sure, continues leading Israel. But, Scripture laments again and again, nothing fundamental has changed. The apparently direct and simple revelation given to Moses turns out to be loaded with paradox. For the creed that Israel is given is lovely except that Israel won't really believe it. The code that Israel is given is great except that Israel won't really obey it. And the worship that Israel is commanded to offer is wonderful except that Israel won't really offer it.

Israel, though, does not know this. And so the nation naively promises "All that the LORD has spoken we will do" (Exodus 19:8) only to discover again and again that they can do (and wish to do) no such thing. Over the centuries, this Bullwinkle Syndrome[1] ("This time for *sure!*") is repeated again and again. Israel vows to *really* keep the covenant repeatedly through the rest of Moses' life. And Joshua's. And the Judges. And so on for three centuries or so after Moses' death until we reach the last Judge of Israel, Samuel. In his days, the nation decides it is tired of having the God of the universe for its King and wishes instead to have some hairy guy with big muscles fill the role (1 Samuel 8). God warns them to be careful of what they wish for because they just might get it. But they insist for the solidly adolescent reason that everybody else has a king so they just gotta have one too. And so God grants their wish with a sort of a sigh.

Curiously, in all the hubbub over monarchy, nobody pauses to notice that God has kept the first part of his promise to Abraham. Phase one is complete. Israel has been formed into a nation by the covenant with Moses as God said would happen. Now the next phase of the promise to Abraham will begin to see fulfillment as the nation be-

---

[1] I am indebted to historian T. David Curp, Ph.D. for this invaluable term.

comes a kingdom. And the Kingdom of the Chosen People will, in its turn, receive further guidance toward its strange destiny.

David

It has been said that God draws straight with crooked lines. This curious process is much in evidence in the inauguration of the fifth and last covenant in the Old Testament. At several crucial junctures in Scripture, the irony is that we humans become convinced that we must beat up God and steal from him something that, had we but known, God intended to give to us all along. A classic and graphic example of this is Jacob, Abraham's thieving grandson, wrestling with an angel and demanding a blessing (Genesis 32:24–32). The man behaved as though God had no intention of blessing him when in reality God had every intention of blessing him and had made that clear before he was ever born (Genesis 25:23).

The same phenomenon is at work in the story of Israel's demand for a king. God fully intended to give Israel a king and a kingdom, but Israel was so sure he wasn't that their demands early and easily acquired a distinctly mutinous tone. So the Father, like any wise parent faced with a sullen teenager demanding the right to smoke cigars like the grown-ups, gave them the whole box of stogies. He picked out for them the tallest, handsomest, coolest dude of a king they ever saw. He was just what everybody wanted. His name was Saul, and he was an instant superstar and overnight success (see 1 Samuel 9–15). But like so many specimens of this sort, Saul therefore became increasingly arrogant, and, at length, forgot God's kindness to him and went about erecting monuments to himself and obeying God when he felt like it. So God promised to take his kingdom away from him and give it, not to the next *People Magazine* hunk provided by a popularity poll, but to the one "I have provided for *myself*". In other words, Saul was the king "everybody" wanted; but the next king would be the one *God* wanted. And so, the Lord who "sees not as man sees" and who looks not on the outward appearance, but on the heart, chooses not another big hairy bruiser, but the runt of Jesse's litter: a kid named David (1 Samuel 9–16).

Since this is a quick survey of the Old Testament we shall not examine here the whole career of David (told in 1 and 2 Samuel). Instead, we will focus on the central moment in the life of David, the covenant God makes with him in 2 Samuel 7.

First, some background. David, after being anointed the future king of Israel by Samuel, briefly becomes a court favorite of Saul's because his fine musicianship eases Saul's increasingly frayed nerves. But David wins fame in battle (this is where the David and Goliath story fits in) and Saul starts to get jealous and increasingly paranoid. The upshot is that David is forced to take it on the lam and spend several years being chased by the increasingly crazed King Saul. But David refuses to kill Saul since Saul is the Lord's Anointed. Eventually Saul and his sons are killed in battle with the Philistines and David is made King over Israel. (See 1 Samuel 16–31 and 2 Samuel 1–6.)

David immediately sets about several projects but one thing in particular interests us here: he captures a Jebusite city called "Jeru-salem" and then fetches the Ark of the Covenant and brings it there with much excitement, fanfare and jubilation.[2] In the midst of this bustle, David then does something remarkable: he dances before the Lord in a linen ephod (a priestly garment), offers burnt offerings and peace offerings before the Lord (a priestly act), blesses the people in the name of the Lord of hosts (another priestly act), and distributes a cake of bread, and, according to some scholars and translations, a portion of wine, to Israel. In short, he assumes the role of a priest-king like Melchizedek in the heart of the city where Melchizedek "King of Salem" and "priest of God Most High" once lived. And to cap this off, he tells the Prophet Nathan that he would like to build a "house" (that is, a temple) for the God of Israel in Jerusalem. This is the prologue to the last great covenant of the Old Testament. For God's reply to David is this:

> "Go and tell my servant David, 'Thus says the LORD: Would you build me a house to dwell in? I have not dwelt in a house since the day I brought up the people of Israel from Egypt to this day, but I have been moving

---

[2] If you are wondering where David fetched the Ark from, 1 Samuel 4–7 tells the tale. Apparently, the ancient Israelites had also seen *Raiders of the Lost Ark* and had believed its fanciful bunkum about the Ark being a cosmic superweapon or surefire lucky rabbit's foot. Several years before Saul's reign, the Israelites had hauled the Ark into battle to ensure their supposed invincibility, only to find that God did not want to be their lucky rabbit's foot but their God. So they lost the battle and the Ark was captured. But the Philistines who captured it also discovered that, though it was not a good luck charm or magical, it *was* more than just a box. Peculiar phenomena surrounded it wherever it went, sending them the distinct message that the God of Israel wanted them to give it back to his people. So they wisely decided to comply. When Israel got it back, they stuck it in a local shrine out in the boondocks and waited to see what they should do next. That is where David got it from when he decided to bring it to Jerusalem.

about in a tent for my dwelling. In all places where I have moved with all the people of Israel, did I speak a word with any of the judges of Israel, whom I commanded to shepherd my people Israel, saying, "Why have you not built me a house of cedar?"' Now therefore thus you shall say to my servant David, 'Thus says the LORD of hosts, I took you from the pasture, from following the sheep, that you should be prince over my people Israel; and I have been with you wherever you went, and have cut off all your enemies from before you; and I will make for you a great name, like the name of the great ones of the earth. And I will appoint a place for my people Israel, and will plant them, that they may dwell in their own place, and be disturbed no more; and violent men shall afflict them no more, as formerly, from the time that I appointed judges over my people Israel; and I will give you rest from all your enemies. Moreover the LORD declares to you that the LORD will make you a house. When your days are fulfilled and you lie down with your fathers, I will raise up your offspring after you, who shall come forth from your body, and I will establish his kingdom. He shall build a house for my name, and I will establish the throne of his kingdom for ever. I will be his father, and he shall be my son. When he commits iniquity, I will chasten him with the rod of men, with the stripes of the sons of men; but I will not take my steadfast love from him, as I took it from Saul, whom I put away from before you. And your house and your kingdom shall be made sure for ever before me; your throne shall be established for ever.'" (2 Samuel 7:5–16)

In short, God says, "You won't build me a house. I'll build you a house! I will establish your dynasty permanently, see it through whatever troubles are ahead and solemnly promise that one of your heirs will always be on

the throne of Israel." This is the covenant with David in
a nutshell and all the rest of the Old Testament is the outworking of this covenant.

Curiously, though "it was in the heart of David" to "build
a house for the name of the LORD, the God of Israel", God
does not grant David's desire. Instead, he tells David that
"your son who shall be born to you shall build the house
for my name" (1 Kings 8:18–19). This prophecy seems at
first to have been completely fulfilled by David's son and
heir, Solomon, when he constructs a magnificent Temple
in Jerusalem to house the Ark and become the central place
for worship. But as time rolls on, the possibility begins to
emerge that God may have meant more by this prophecy
than meets the eye. Here's why:

The Davidic Covenant is Still Not Enough

The trouble with the Davidic Covenant, like the Mosaic Covenant, is that it is still inadequate to fulfill all the
promises given to Abraham. God's family has grown from
a couple (in Adam and Eve) to a family (in Noah) to a tribe
(in Abraham) to a nation (in Moses) to a kingdom ruling
other nations (in David). But God has not yet blessed all
the nations of the earth as he promised Abraham.

Nor has another promise been accomplished — the one
made to the serpent that the "seed of the woman" would
crush the serpent's head. Far from it, the serpent is doing very well, thank you. And so, shortly after David receives his wonderful promises from God, the serpent strikes
David's heel and he commits the gravest sin of his life:
adultery with Bathsheba and the murder of her husband,

Uriah (see 2 Samuel 11:1–12:23). Nathan confronts David and David repents, but the Lord, though he forgives David, nevertheless utters a terrible prophecy against the House he has promised to establish: "Now therefore the sword shall never depart from your house, because you have despised me, and have taken the wife of Uriah the Hittite to be your wife" (2 Samuel 12:10). That sword slices its way through the rest of the Old Testament, ripping open David's family in vicious dynastic disputes. It cleaves Israel in a civil war that produces two kingdoms: Israel in the north and Judah in the south. It divides the faithful from kings who abandon God and persecute his followers. It is swung by Assyrians who annihilate the Northern Kingdom of Israel and come within bowshot of the gates of Judah's capitol, Jerusalem. It divides apostate children from faithful parents and repentant children from their sinful elders.

Meanwhile, as Israel and Judah are slowly experiencing the rot, God sends the prophets. He sends men like Elijah and Elisha (whose stories are told in 1 and 2 Kings). He sends Isaiah, Jeremiah, Ezekiel and several others whose books we have plus many others whose prophecies do not get written down. And the theme of the prophets is always the same: Return to the Lord and his covenant with Moses. The prophets fight a long, slow rearguard action against the encroaching night of lawlessness and divine judgement. God sets them the terrible task of trying to exhort a faithless people to faithfulness. And, in gratitude for their valuable contributions to the public welfare, their countrymen drop them down wells, saw them in two, spit them on swords, behead them and generally make them feel unwelcome. Meanwhile, as the centuries pass, the sky becomes darker and darker till the storm finally breaks.

Finally, inexorably, the sword Nathan prophesied to David's house is brought down one last time with over-whelming force on Judah by Nebuchadnezzar, the great king of Babylon, who fulfills all the warnings of the prophets by destroying Jerusalem and its Temple, deport-ing the population, and leaving the land desolate for 70 years in what is known as the "Babylonian Captivity."

All, it would seem, is lost but for this: the prophets God sent had promised *judgment* for David's house, not annihi-lation. For the Lord had promised through Nathan "When he commits iniquity, I will chasten him with the rod of men, with the stripes of the sons of men; *but I will not take my steadfast love from him*" (2 Samuel 7:14–15). And so, though prophets spent their words, their blood, and the next four centuries from the death of David to the Babylo-nian Captivity calling the house of David and the kingdom of Judah back to the covenant with Moses and warning of the dire consequences of unrepentance, they never de-clared that Judah would be eradicated. On the contrary, coupled with the harshest rebukes, they also remind Judah of the promise God has made — the promise that David's throne "shall be established forever." And so, when the blow falls and Nebuchadnezzar sends Judah into captivity, the prophets assure the dispirited refugees that the nation shall be restored, that "in that day I will raise up the booth of David that is fallen and repair its breaches, and raise up its ruins, and rebuild it as in the days of old" (Amos 9:11).

And, in the end, it is raised up again. The promise to Judah is fulfilled and many captives return. God sends new prophets to exhort Judah to restoration (see, for in-stance, Haggai and Zechariah). Under the inspiration of such prophets, and with the leadership of faithful men (such as Ezra and Nehemiah), many Jews ("Jew" derives from "Judah") restore fallen Jerusalem, begin to rebuild the Temple, and rededicate themselves to the covenant with Moses. Meanwhile, others remain in exile and begin to spread through the length and breadth of the ancient world and form communities everywhere.

But three things linger in the air, unresolved.

The first is the mystery of the promise to Abraham. Just how is it that all the nations of the earth shall be blessed through Abraham? Especially, when it often seems that "the nations conspire, / and the peoples plot in vain. / The kings of the earth set themselves, / and the rulers take counsel together, / against the LORD" (Psalm 2:1–2). The Jewish people are now weaker politically than they have ever been and, as history rolls on, are increasingly confronted with the fact that this situation is not going to improve. The Jews who are dispersed all over the ancient world are a distinct (and often rather unpopular) minority in every community outside Judea. It had seemed that the blessing of Abraham was going to be given the world via a conquering Davidic empire. The hopes for empire are gone forever. So now what?

This brings us to our second unresolved mystery at the end of the Old Testament: the mystery of the promise to David. Where is the heir — the Son of David — who is to sit on the throne of Israel? Who is this mysterious Son of David? The Jewish nation ruminates on this as her political fortunes continue to wane under a series of foreign dominations. To be sure, the nation never gives up holding on to the covenants and promises given her. And when foreign powers attempt to erase the heritage God has entrusted to the Jews, they find themselves facing opposition, not simply from Jewish arms, but from a mysteriously Providential power that makes sure the revelation — and the nation — is preserved. This is the lesson of books like Judith, Esther, and 1 and 2 Maccabees. But preserved for what?

The Jewish people waits . . . and waits . . . and waits, like Father Abraham waited for the birth of Isaac. And while she waits she too is slowly made ready as Abraham was. As the centuries roll on, she ruminates on various things, including the mysterious words of the prophets concerning a coming figure (called variously, "the Son of Man," the "Servant of the Lord," "the Prophet," "the Star out of Jacob" and various other titles[3]) who seems to be promised by God to somehow deliver Israel from oppression. The general conviction grows that Jews have yet to wait for some future figure — the Anointed One or "Messiah" — who will bring some sort of resolution to all the covenants, make sense of all the tumult of history since then, and "utter what has been hidden since the foundation of the world" (Psalm 78:2).

And while she ruminates on this, the Jewish nation also ponders, particularly in her prophets, her long struggle with the tension of the Mosaic covenant — the creed, code and cult which must be kept and yet can't be kept. What is she to make of this strange burden that God has laid on her back? How is she to resolve the apparently impossible contradiction of it all?

The Jewish people, agonizing through centuries of suffering, prayer and thought to which the world owes a debt

---

[3] The titles listed here derive from Daniel 7:13, Isaiah 42:1–9, 49:1–7, 50:4–11, 52:13–53:12, Deuteronomy 18:15 and Numbers 24:17). There are numerous other messianic allusions all through the Old Testament.

that can never be paid, is brought by God in the fullness of time to face one last unresolved mystery through the words of the prophet Jeremiah:

> "Behold, the days are coming, says the LORD, when I will make a new covenant with the house of Israel and the house of Judah, not like the covenant which I made with their fathers when I took them by the hand to bring them out of the land of Egypt, my covenant which they broke, though I was their husband, says the LORD. But this is the covenant which I will make with the house of Israel after those days, says the LORD: I will put my law within them, and I will write it upon their hearts; and I will be their God, and they shall be my people. . . ." (Jeremiah 31:31–33)

So some sixth covenant remains yet to made, a covenant which will not just tell us what is wrong with us (as the law of Moses does) but change us and "write the law on our hearts." But what it will look like and how it will happen, nobody really knows. The Jewish people must wait for the fullness of time, for the fulfillment of the promises, and for the coming of Messiah.

4

Light of the Gentiles, Glory of Israel

Right in the middle of these things stands up an enormous exception. It is quite unlike anything else. It is a thing final like the trump of doom, though it is also a piece of good news; or news that seems too good to be true. It is nothing less than the loud assertion that this mysterious maker of the world has visited his world in person. It declares that really and even recently, or right in the middle of historic times, there did walk into the world this original invisible being; about whom the thinkers make theories and mythologists hand down myths; the Man Who Made the World. That such a higher personality exists behind all things has indeed always been implied by all the best thinkers, as well as by all the most beautiful legends. But nothing of this sort had ever been implied in any of them. It is simply false to say that the other sages and heroes had claimed to be that mysterious master and maker, of whom the world had dreamed and disputed. Not one of them had ever claimed to be anything of the sort. Not one of their sects or schools had ever claimed that they had claimed to be anything of the sort. The most that any religious prophet had said was that he was the true servant of such a being. The most that any visionary had ever said was that men might catch glimpses of the glory of that spiritual being; or much more often of lesser spiritual beings. The most that any primitive myth had ever suggested was that the Creator was present at the creation. But that the Creator was present at scenes a little subsequent to the supper-parties of Horace, and talked with tax-collectors and government officials in the detailed daily life of the Roman Empire, and that this fact continued to be firmly asserted by the whole of that great civilization for more than a thousand years — that is something utterly unlike anything else in nature. It is the one great startling statement that man has made since he spoke his first articulate word, instead of barking like a dog. Its unique character can be used as an argument against it as well as for it. It would be easy to concentrate on it as a case of isolated insanity; but it makes nothing but dust and nonsense of comparative religion.

— G. K. Chesterton

Israel has preserved the revelation entrusted to it by God. In the meantime, what has the rest of humanity been up to since Noah?

Well, like Israel, the rest of humankind, sons and daughters of Adam and Eve all, are struggling with the afflictions of our fallen condition just like Israel. And so, ancient history is, in part, a chronicle of wars, deportations, enslavement, and various barbarities (much like modern history). But that is not all. As St. Paul says, "[I]s God the God of Jews only? Is he not the God of Gentiles also? Yes, of Gentiles also, since God is one" (Romans 3:29–30). And since God is the God of all and not just of a particular nation at the eastern end of the Mediterranean, he has been preparing the Gentiles, as he has been preparing Israel, for his sixth and final covenant. But that preparation looks very different.

As we noted previously, the last covenant made with all humanity was through Noah. In the ages after Noah, the Fall continues to have its ruinous effects on the human race, but the Spirit of God also continues to work, drawing the world slowly toward light (Isaiah 60:1–3). And so, the human race, always conscious that there is something out of whack with itself, invents a thousand religious, philosophical, mystical, and political strategies for trying to make sense of the world. This welter of strategies was neither wholly wrong nor particularly right. Operating by natural revelation, the ancient world was very sensibly theistic, yet almost without exception crazily *poly*theistic. In the absence of the revelation vouchsafed to Israel, human beings did what human beings do: they told stories. Some of the stories tapped into very deep wellsprings of truth and gave the world profound insights in the great myths. Some of the stories were silly and even the tellers of those stories knew it. Some of the stories were dark and imagined gods far less noble than their creatures. But the thing they had in common was that they were stories. That is, they were, as Chesterton observed, attempts to reach God through the imagination. Where the law of Moses offered to Israel the creed of a God who revealed himself through historic acts, the stories offered the guesses, dreams — and nightmares — of poets.

Along with the stories were the mysteries. That is, a vast array of religious rituals and practices centered around the deep human impulse to offer sacrifice and to be cleansed.

Just what was to be sacrificed varied from a pinch of incense to bulls to children. Likewise, just why we needed to sacrifice was not altogether clear. Here again, absent real revelation the human race just made things up as it went along and got things partly right and, often, horribly wrong (under the influence of the demonic, as St. Paul tells us in 1 Corinthians 10:20–21). Occasionally, the mysteries, like the stories, had flashes of insight into some primordial truth. So for instance, the cult of Osiris in Egypt centered around the idea of a god who dies, and somehow, through this, gains kingship.[1] In Norse mythology as well, Balder dies as "myself sacrificed to Myself."[2] And in Mithraism, the tale is told of a great warrior hero who killed a wild bull and from its blood sprang life and grain. Mithras is worshipped with the cry, "You saved us by shedding the eternal blood."[3] In various and sundry forms of ritual worship of various deities all over the ancient world, there emerges a number of dim notions similar to the blood sacrifices of Israel: the idea that the shedding of blood is somehow necessary to setting the world aright or, as Israel was told, that "the blood is the life" (Deuteronomy 12:23). Here again, the human race tended to recapitulate in a by guess and by golly way what Israel was receiving by revelation from God.

Finally, in addition to these more murky and visceral in-

---

[1] Everett Ferguson, *Backgrounds of Early Christianity, Second Edition* (Grand Rapids: Eerdmans, 1993), p. 254.

[2] "I know that I hung on the gallows for nine nights, wounded with the spear as a sacrifice to Odin, myself offered to Myself." (Hávamál, I.10 in *Corpus Poeticum Boreal*; stanza 139 in Hildebrand's *Lieder der Alteren Edda*, 1922).

[3] Ferguson, *Backgrounds of Early Christianity*, p. 275.

sights, there is the drive in various places (most notably in Greece and later, Rome) not merely to tell stories or engage in mysteries, but to codify and make rational, philosophical sense of the world. This enterprise is fueled by many ancient thinkers from Buddha in the Far East to Plato in the West, but all these philosophers and thinkers have in common the desire to come up with some way of systematizing existence and making sense of it. They all have in common the same reality of conscience known to Eskimos, three-year-olds and you and me and they all attempt to find some way to obey this fundamental demand of the moral law that we Do the Right Thing. Some, notably in Babylon, are aware of a dim connection between man and the created world and attempt to read the pattern of that connection by guesses about the meanings of the stars. In short, here again, the human race, absent the Mosaic law vouchsafed to Israel, responds higgledy-piggledy to the law written on the heart. And, like Israel, they experience some success and a great deal of failure.

In short then, Gentile humanity labors without the benefit of direct revelation and under the yoke of the Fall like all human beings. In God's Providence, Gentiles recapitulate in the vast and muddled welter of their stories, mysteries and philosophies a smudged, confused, erroneous and sometimes diabolically distorted sketch that nonetheless winds up bearing some surprising resemblances to the creed, code and cult which God reveals to Israel through Moses. But because the human race is fallen the human mind, like the human heart, is so addled that the attempt is often very confused and erroneous indeed. And even where it approaches real insights and does not trail off into nonsense, Gentile humanity, like Jewish humanity, suffers from the same difficulty of failing to live up to its own highest truths.

And so, in the fullness of time, the whole of the human race, both Jew and Gentile, toils though ancient history until it reaches a point of crisis. In Judaism, the crisis is met in several ways. One is mere apostasy. Some Jews simply abandon the practice of the faith (1 Maccabees 1). Another way is Pharisaism: some Jews simply reject anything with a Gentile taint and try to live in ultra-purity. A third way, more amenable to us moderns, is the attempt by some Jews to understand what is of God in Gentile culture.

Several specimens of this attempt are found in the text of the Old Testament itself. Job, for instance, is notable as a Gentile who suffers horrendous tragedy, not because he is forsaken of God, but because he is one of God's special favorites. Besides being a profound meditation on the meaning of suffering, Job has a particularly pointed moral to a Jewish audience if it is jingoistically tempted to read too much into the plight of this unfortunate Gentile. For Job, despite his status as a Gentile, is vindicated by God himself and praised by the Almighty as "my servant." The Jewish writer of Job is, among many other things, clearly exploring what God might be up to with the good members of "the nations."

Likewise, the book of Ruth goes out of its way to give the story of a pious woman from the neighboring Moabite peoples who, though not of Israel, nonetheless enters into the promise of Israel by her faithfulness to her Israelite kinswoman, Naomi. Ruth ends up marrying into the family of a man named Boaz and, as the author carefully notes, becomes an ancestor of none other than King David himself.

Similarly, the book of Jonah, one of the minor prophets, tells the tale of a prophet who does everything in his power to avoid prophesying to the Gentiles at Nineveh (admittedly not a lovely group of people — the Assyrians of Nineveh were the Nazis of the ancient world). The author makes it clear that Jonah is avoiding the task, not because he is afraid the Assyrians won't listen to him, but because he fears they will. Jonah *wants* Nineveh destroyed. But, as the author shows, God has other plans. He wants Gentiles — even Assyrians — to be saved from destruction. He sees something worth saving even outside the covenant people. And he leaves Israel to cogitate on that fact.

This sort of cogitation goes on through the history of Israel. One notable practitioner of it after the completion of the Old Testament books is a North African Jewish writer named Philo (30 B.C.–50 A.D.), who takes some of the ideas of the Greek philosopher Plato and tries to reconcile them with the teaching of Judaism.

> Philo has an elaborate *Logos* speculation, and this has attracted students of the New Testament and Christology to his writings. According to Philo the Logos was the mind or reason of God, the locus of the ideas of Platonic philosophy. The Logos was God in his rational aspect, but the Logos also functions as the head of the hierarchy of intermediaries between the world and God.[4]

Philo, feeling his way along the edges of the boundary between Judaism and Greek philosophy, makes some educated guesses about what God, in his Providence, might be up to among the Gentiles as their best teachers (like

---

[4] Ferguson, *Backgrounds of Early Christianity*, p. 451.

Plato) search for truth. He is not afraid to "test everything and hold fast what is good" (1 Thessalonians 5:21) even when a thing originates among the Gentiles. And as he is feeling his way, making his best guesses about the Platonic Logos as the expression of the mind of God, he tosses off a curious flippancy: "God would sooner change into a man than man into a god."[5] He meant nothing serious by it but, as is the way with wise and honest people, he wound up saying more than he realized.

But though Philo in North Africa is creeping so close to guessing the nature of the sixth covenant that he almost trips over it, Messianic Judaism in Judea has a more distinctly politicized tint. For Judea is being ground under the Roman boot, and that crisis is manifested in a widespread longing for the coming Messiah to appear as a resurgent Davidic King and beat up the Romans. Some try to hurry the coming of Messiah via various revolts and uprisings (which were often put down with ferocious violence). Meanwhile, in the Gentile lands, this same sense of world crisis was expressed in even more confused ways.

First, Gentile humanity was beginning to despair of its stories. This does not mean that it ceased telling them, only that it was beginning to cease being nourished by them. By the time of Christ, Gentile humanity in the Mediterranean world was inexorably making the same depressing discovery that comes to all children: not only Santa Claus, but Persephone, Osiris, Isis, Diana and the rest of the mythological folk did not really exist. Their stories were fun when the race was younger. But they did not

---

[5] Philo, *Embassy to Gaius*, 16.118.

satisfy for they were not real. They were based on a mood of rude good health and imagination, not on truth. And when systematic thought (nearly always systematic thought from Gentile philosophers) asked probing questions about them, it was quickly obvious that the stories were only stories, however delightful they might be. This sad and slow discovery of what, in their hearts, they already knew, was coupled with another curious phenomenon. In a dim and half-understood way, some of the best poets were, in the middle of this despair, able to give voice to a curiously messianic-sounding hopefulness:

Now is the last age of the song of Cumae; and the great line of the centuries begins new. Now the Virgin [Justice] returns, the reign of Saturn returns [a new Golden age]; now a new generation descends from heaven on high. Only do thou, pure Lucina, smile on the birth of the child, under whom the iron brood shall first cease, and a golden race spring up throughout the world! Thine own Apollo now is King!

And in thy consulship, Pollio, yea in thine, shall this glorious age begin, and the mighty months commence their march; under thy sway, any lingering traces of our guilt shall become void, and release the earth from its continual dread. He shall have the gift of divine life, shall see heroes mingled with gods, and shall himself be seen of them, and shall sway a world to which his father's virtues have brought peace.

But for thee, child, shall the earth untilled pour forth . . . . [There follows the description of prosperity and abundance.]

Enter on thy high honors — the hour will soon be here — O thou dear offspring of the gods, mighty seat of Jupiter to be! Behold the world bowing with its massive dome

— earth and expanse of sea and heaven's depth! Behold all things exalt in the age that is at hand![6]

This curious sense of huge and exalted expectancy, out of all proportion to the actual subject of the poem (i.e., the birth of a Roman aristocrat's baby) reflects well the curiously heightened anticipation in the Gentile mind of some imminent "age that is at hand" when the "iron brood" (that is, the present human race) would cease and the golden race (whatever that was to be) would appear. "Guilt" would become void and "the gift of divine life" bestowed — all through the birth of a child. As with Philo, Vergil (the Roman author of the poem) accidentally teeters so close to the sixth covenant that later Christian readers would speculate that God may have been giving him mysterious prophetic insights.[7] Once again, we get the odd impression that the Gentiles are, in their own haphazard fashion, being prepared by God for some great Advent even in the midst of their growing despair.

And the despair was growing. For Gentile humanity was not only beginning to despair of its stories, it was beginning to despair of its mysteries as well. Slowly but surely, it was discovering that the difficulty with trying to reach God through the imagination alone is that one tends to end up worshiping creatures and losing sight of their Creator. Gentile humanity, like the writer of Genesis, had a very good insight: Creation was good. But without the revela-

---

[6] Vergil, *Eclogues* 4:4–52, trans. H. R. Fairclough in Loeb Classical Library. Cited in Ferguson, *Backgrounds of Early Christianity*, *Second Edition*, p. 104.

[7] S. Benko, "Vergil's Fourth Eclogue in Christian Interpretation," ANRW II, Principat, 31.1 (Berlin, 1980), pp. 646–705.

tion given Israel, it was fatally easy to pass from saying
Creation was good to saying Creation was God. This error was recapitulated incessantly outside the Jewish nation
(and often within it as well, as the Golden Calf attests).
But this error, like all error, leads ultimately to frustration, for it does not satisfy. And this frustration led, not
to the cessation, but to the frantic multiplication of mystery cults in the increasingly desperate hope that, this time,
the old feelings of revelry in mere Nature would return.
But the old feelings of piety and rude pagan jollity in nature worship were fading. Nature was good, but it was
not worth our worship. When we tried to make it so, we
kept finding that however much we admired the butterfly
or the singing bird, we found it much easier to imitate
the tiger, the rutting dog or the leech. For a great number
of people, this despair of childlike joy led not to insights
but to squalor. Like so many disillusioned ciphers today
who drool and watch pathetic people beat each other up
on tabloid TV, the Gentiles consoled themselves with glad-
iators killing each other in the arena. But others, aware as
we are of our cultural decay, were slowly coming to contemplate the prospect that we might have made a fundamental mistake by worshiping Creation and forgetting the
Creator — whoever that might be.

Round about the same time as these developments, the
philosophers and thinkers were facing their own despair
as well. As Chesterton writes:

> Something similar was happening to that intellectual aris-
> tocracy of antiquity that had been walking about and talk-
> ing at large ever since Socrates and Pythagoras. They be-
> gan to betray to the world the fact that they were walking
> in a circle and saying the same thing over and over again.

Philosophy began to be a joke; it also began to be a bore. . .
Everywhere the sages had generated into sophists; that is,
into hired rhetoricians or askers of riddles. It is one of
the symptoms of this that the sage begins to turn not only
into a sophist but into a magician. A touch of Oriental
occultism is very much appreciated in the best houses. As
the philosopher is already a society entertainer, he may as
well also be a conjurer.[8]

As Israel had failed to keep its law, so Gentile humanity
was failing to keep even the fragmentary bits of law written
on its heart. The chattering classes were beginning to abandon the pursuit of wisdom and opting for the pursuit of
cleverness in the same hour that the mysteries were starting
to die and the stories were being outgrown. By the time of
Christ the whole of the Mediterranean world had achieved
the project toward which all of antiquity had been straining: a well-rounded, complete and civilized world. And it
was not enough, not nearly enough, to satisfy the human
soul. Again, to quote Chesterton:

It is essential to recognize that the Roman Empire was
recognized as the highest achievement of the human race;
and also as the broadest. . . There was nothing left that
could conquer Rome; but there was also nothing left that
could improve it. It was the strongest thing that was growing weak. It was the best thing that was going to the bad.
It is necessary to insist again and again that many civili-
sations had met in one civilisation of the Mediterranean
Sea; that it was already universal with a stale and ster-
ile universality. The peoples had pooled their resources

---

[8] G. K. Chesterton, *The Everlasting Man* (Garden City: Image, 1955),
p. 166.

and still there was not enough. The empires had gone into partnership and they were bankrupt. No philosopher who was really philosophical could think anything except that, in that central sea, the wave of the world had risen to its highest, seeming to touch the stars. But the wave was already stooping; for it was only the wave of the world.[9]

And so, by the beginning of the first century A.D. there had descended upon Jews and Gentiles alike the growing and powerful sense that the time was fast approaching when this mysterious crisis was to reach a mysterious climax. By his providential care, he who is God of the Gentiles as well as the Jews had brought the human race to the point of readiness for something of which the world itself did not guess. Just as Israel was waiting for the coming of Messiah, so the civilization of Gentiles beyond Israel had arrived willy-nilly at the dim, half-perceived and visceral awareness that it was standing on tiptoe waiting for . . . it knew not what.

It was into the heart of this civilization — into the Athens of the mysteries, myths, and philosophers — that there walked one day an itinerant Jewish preacher. Among these sophisticated and world-weary cosmopolitan Greeks (who, as the preacher's amused companion remarked, "spent their time in nothing except telling or hearing something new") he wandered for a while until his eye fell on a monument dedicated by the Athenians, in a sort of bet-hedging half-hopefulness, "To an Unknown God." Here, it seemed to him, was the hope and despair of the non-Jewish children of Noah focused to a pinpoint. And so, as he had been sent to do, the preacher stood up and declared:

---

[9] Chesterton, *The Everlasting Man*, p. 167.

"Men of Athens, I perceive that in every way you are very religious. For as I passed along, and observed the objects of your worship, I found also an altar with this inscription, 'To an unknown god.' What therefore you worship as unknown, this I proclaim to you. The God who made the world and everything in it, being Lord of heaven and earth, does not live in shrines made by man, nor is he served by human hands, as though he needed anything, since he himself gives to all men life and breath and everything. And he made from one every nation of men to live on all the face of the earth, having determined allotted periods and the boundaries of their habitation, that they should seek God, in the hope that they might feel after him and find him. Yet he is not far from each one of us, for 'In him we live and move and have our being'; as even some of your poets have said, 'For we are indeed his offspring.'

Being then God's offspring, we ought not to think that the Deity is like gold, or silver, or stone, a representation by the art and imagination of man. The times of ignorance God overlooked, but now he commands all men everywhere to repent, because he has fixed a day on which he will judge the world in righteousness by a man whom he has appointed, and of this he has given assurance to all men by raising him from the dead." (Acts 17:22–31)

Who Do You Say That I Am?

The preacher turned out to be a man named Paul from Tarsus (in modern day Turkey), and the man who would "judge the world" and who had been "raised from the dead," according to Paul, was an obscure rabbi on the eastern fringe of the Empire who, about twenty years previously, had been executed on somewhat vague charges of being a nuisance during the tenure of the Roman Prefect Pontius Pilate. Yet Paul never spoke of that man as though he were dead. Rather he believed in him, not as though he were merely a great teacher, or healer, or prophet, nor as though he were a martyr, but as though he was the living God of Israel.

How did Paul become convinced of such an extraordinary thing? Well, for one thing, according to Paul himself, that unusual man met him on a road near Damascus several years after his execution by Pilate and told him to visit places like Athens and tell them he was alive (Acts 9:1–19; 22:1–21; 26:4–23). Of course, Paul might have just been an isolated lunatic — but for the fact that he wasn't isolated. There were others — many others — who said the same thing. And the story they told boils down to this: God had at long last inaugurated his sixth and final covenant, a covenant which turned out to be not only with the Jews but with all the scattered children of Adam and Noah as well. He had, at long last, "remember[ed] his holy covenant, the oath which he swore to our father Abraham" (Luke 1:72–73) and had, through the Jews, sent a Messiah into the world so that all the nations of the earth would be blessed. He had, at long last, fulfilled the law and the prophets and brought to fruition all that he had promised his servant David. But most extraordinary of all, that Messiah had turned out to be not just a man sent by God, but God himself in human flesh.

This, in a nutshell, is who the early Christians proclaimed Jesus of Nazareth to be. On this claim hinges the entire faith of Christendom. It is well, therefore, given the enormity of that claim, to pin down the evidence for it.

Many people, especially today, have the idea that we can account for Jesus in some way that is simpler than the Catholic explanation. Some say he was a great prophet. Some hail him as the first Marxist. Some call him a wise teacher like many others. Some think him a figment of the imagination, cobbled together from pagan myths. Some think him a manifestation of the divine principle within all men and women, no different from us but merely "enlightened."

In fact, there are all sorts of explanations of who Jesus really is. Let us briefly examine what Jesus himself claimed and what eyewitnesses to his life came to believe. After all, Jesus himself bade his disciples to do just this in Matthew 16:13–15:

> Now when Jesus came into the district of Caesarea Philippi, he asked his disciples, "Who do men say that the Son of man is?" And they said, "Some say John the Baptist, others say Elijah, and others Jeremiah or one of the prophets." He said to them, "But who do you say that I am?"

The first thing to notice from this passage is that there has never been a shortage of opinion about Jesus' identity. Even in the time of the apostles, every Tom, Dick and Harry was ready to offer his personal theory about the Galilean. The second thing to notice is that Jesus demands his disciples make up their minds about him and not waffle around forever listening to the latest opinion polls.

That is wise, because Jesus, both by his words and deeds, leaves no doubt as to who he claims to be: the incarnate Son of God. This is why, moments after the question above was asked, this exchange took place:

Simon Peter replied, "You are the Christ, the Son of the living God." And Jesus answered him, "Blessed are you, Simon Bar-Jona! For flesh and blood has not revealed this to you, but my Father who is in heaven." (Matthew 16:16–17)

Jesus clearly claimed to be "Christ" and "Son of the Living God." By his life, miracles, death and resurrection, he convinced his followers of the truth of this claim. But, of course, we still hear "alternative explanations." How do they stack up with the record? Here are some of the more popular alternative explanations:

Nice Teacher

This theory holds that Jesus was not really divine, but was just a sage and moral exemplar from whom we could learn a lot about tolerance and so forth.

The difficulty here is the little matter of his claim to deity. Sages don't claim to be God. Yet Jesus of Nazareth claims for himself the name "I AM" which is the very name of God in the Hebrew language (John 8:58). He proclaims himself "Lord of the Sabbath." (Mark 2:28) and forgives sins (and in so doing implies he is the judge of the human race) (Mark 2:1–12; Matthew 25:31–46). He names himself "the Son" who alone knows the Father and who alone can make the Father known (Luke 10:22). And he reasserts these claims when he is on trial for his life (Mark 14:61–62). Merely human sages don't act this way. God Incarnate does.

Guru to the Jews

Lately it has become fashionable to explain away Jesus' claim to deity by saying that it was intended "in an Eastern sense." By this, it is meant that Jesus was really a Hindu or Shirley MacLaine devotee asserting his "God consciousness" in an attempt to awaken this same consciousness in his benighted peers. This theory holds that Jesus did not mean that he and he alone is the God of Israel and the Transcendent Creator of Heaven and Earth but rather that he meant we are *all* God ourselves if we but realize it.

The problems with this theory are numerous, the main one being that there is not a scrap of evidence to support the contention that Jesus was anything other than a Jew immersed in the Scripture and Tradition of Israel. So far from revolutionizing Judaism into a religion that identifies God with the world, Jesus endlessly affirms that God is *Lord* of heaven and earth, not that he *is* heaven and earth as this theory asserts (Luke 10:21). He does not speak of God as identical with Creation; he speaks of him in an utterly Jewish sense as Transcendent Creator, Judge and Father (Matthew 19:4; 6:14–15). Likewise, he does not say sin is unreal. Rather, he constantly reminds his disciples they are sinners incapable of accomplishing salvation or anything else apart from him (John 15:5). He draws a continual distinction between himself and us, with frequent reminders that we are sinful, but he is without sin; we are from below, but he is from above (John 8:1–11; 8:23). He insists that the way to life is not via self-affirmation of our own intrinsic divinity but self-denial for his sake, who alone is one with the Father (Matthew 16:24–26; John 10:30). In short, he is not calling us to realize our own deity, but to recognize his. This again makes sense if he is God Incarnate, but not if he is a Guru.

Swindler

The stark realization that Jesus really does insist on our sinfulness and contrast it with his sinlessness is deeply offensive to the modern egalitarian soul. When moderns learn that the documents really do reflect this, some immediately seize on yet another explanation of who Jesus really was: a religious charlatan who succeeded in starting a local cult of worship round himself in the hopes of gaining earthly fame and fortune under a cloak of charismatic leadership.

The problem with this theory is that its fiercest opponents are themselves non-Christians. Proponents of the Swindler Theory must argue not against Christianity, but against Christianity's bitterest enemies such as Marx and Nietzsche. Their complaint about Christ was not against his forceful will to power but against his *meekness,* "slave morality" and "failure" to demand revolt among the oppressed masses and his "weak" counsels to turn the other cheek; counsels he clearly kept himself.

The mystery for adherents of the Swindler Theory is just what earthly treasure Jesus was supposed to have wanted. Political glory? He is so politically unassertive that he flees into the desert when people try to make him king (John 6:15). Similarly, he makes speeches (such as his Bread of Life discourse) (John 6:25–60) guaranteed to repulse and offend all but the most die-hard supporters. He also does everything he can to conceal his miracles (Mark 5:43, 7:36; Luke 5:14). And strangest of all, he keeps the most disreputable company at the very worst of times. Surrounding

oneself with men who smell like fish, or with Mary Magda-
lene, Simon the Zealot, Zacchaeus the Tax Collector, and
a whole raft of prostitutes, pimps, mentally ill, demon-
possessed and otherwise unsavory people is not the way
to impress constituents, gain support from Big Money or
overwhelm the Honchos in Jerusalem with one's promise
as a Great Man. One is usually careful about the impression
one wishes to make with Top People.

Jesus, however, was a remarkably incautious Swindler,
if Swindler he was. And for a clever Swindler bent on
improving his earthly fortunes, he seemed particularly at
pains to make sure that those who thought the least of him
— and had the power to do something about it — would
kill him. Those bent on earthly power, on trial for their
lives, usually haggle about fine points of law and want to
obfuscate terms by delay tactics. They want to spend a lot
of time fussing about what the meaning of "is" is. Jesus,
in contrast, is breathtakingly direct — and in a way that is
certain, not to save his life, but guarantee his execution.

> Again the high priest asked him, "Are you the Christ, the
> Son of the Blessed?"
> "I am," said Jesus. (Mark 14:61–62)

* * *

> And Pilate asked him, "Are you the king of the Jews?"
> And he answered him, "You have said so." (Mark 15:2)

If someone can see a swindler craving earthly delights
at work in this confession which guaranteed crucifixion, it
is difficult to see how they do it. The evidence points, for
most people of common sense, not to a desire for power
and domination, but to Christ's own claim that he already
had all power and was here to give it (and his life) away

to whoever would listen to him. Once again, the evidence squares with Christ's claim to be the "Son of the living God."

Which leaves one alternative to the Catholic explanation open:

Mad Man

This theory, in a nutshell, is that Jesus was a nut who thought he was God and had some sort of weird death wish. It was, by the way, something like this theory that was adopted by his contemporaries and even by some of his family members (Mark 3:21–22). But this theory, like all the others, runs aground on certain hard facts.

The first fact is the words and deeds of Jesus himself. For instance, the Sermon on the Mount (Matthew 5–7) does not exactly resemble the gibberings of the daffy. Likewise, the sharp and canny analysis of the elite in Matthew 23 is not reflective of madness. So too his savvy reply in the debate over paying taxes to Caesar (Mark 12:13–17). And the breathtaking light-footedness of his answer to those who wanted to stone the woman taken in adultery also bespeaks a mind that is extraordinarily balanced, not unbalanced (John 8:1–11). He is lucid, fresh, ironic and humorous in ways simply not given to the morbidly self-absorbed and psychotic.

Which highlights the curious ambiguity of his appointment with death. For though he aims for it with unbreakable resolve we never get the impression that he *desires* it like a morbid romantic. He weeps at the grave of Lazarus (John 11:35). He sweats blood on the eve of his own death and begs God to be spared (Luke 22:41–44). But though he hates death, he submits to it. In fact, he looks like a man *under orders*. This does not at all square with the picture of a lunatic. It does square rather disturbingly with the idea that Jesus is the Son of God who came into the world to destroy death in obedience to the Father.

And so, in the end, we return to that moment when Jesus confronted his disciples asking, "Who do you say that I am?" (Matthew 16:15). And as we look at that question again, we begin to see C. S. Lewis' point that

> The historical difficulty of giving for the life, sayings and influence of Jesus any explanation that is not harder than the Christian explanation is very great. The discrepancy between the depth and sanity and (let me add) *shrewdness* of his moral teaching and the rampant megalomania which must lie behind his theological teaching unless he is indeed God, has never been satisfactorily got over.[10]

Nor does escape get easier when we pass from examining Jesus' claim to deity to the great miracle that capped his life and established that claim: his own resurrection. For the problem of finding a better explanation than the Catholic one for what happened on the first Easter when Jesus was "designated Son of God in power according to the Spirit of holiness by his resurrection from the dead" (Romans 1:4) is even more overwhelming than the problem of finding alternative explanations for his claims of deity. It is this enormous miracle upon which the apostles hung all their hopes, their good news, and ultimately their lives. As St. Paul said,

---

[10] C. S. Lewis, *Miracles* (New York: Macmillan, 1947), pp. 108–109.

[I]f Christ has not been raised, then our preaching is in
vain and your faith is in vain. We are even found to be
misrepresenting God, because we testified of God that he
raised Christ, whom he did not raise if it is true that the
dead are not raised. For if the dead are not raised, then
Christ has not been raised. If Christ has not been raised,
your faith is futile and you are still in your sins. Then
those also who have fallen asleep in Christ have perished.
If for this life only we have hoped in Christ, we are of all
men most to be pitied. (1 Corinthians 15:14–19)

If the announcement of the resurrection is bogus, how
do we account for the disciples who make the claim?

The cheapest way to account for them is to declare them
fanatics who hysterically hallucinated the whole thing. Un-
fortunately, as with most cheap things, you get what you
pay for. And the evidence to back this claim up is mighty
skimpy.

The apostles actually appear in the record as a group
of people who, so far from being wild-eyed hysterics, are
pretty slow on the uptake. Again and again, Jesus groans in
frustration at them, "Do you *still* not understand?" (Mark
8:21). They are constantly rebuked, not for their fanatical
faith in him, but for their dull incomprehension and pedes-
trian failure to have even a little trust. So far from reading
undue significance into things, the disciples often display
an oxen incomprehension of even the simplest teaching and
a positive resistance to some of the harder ones (Mark 8:16;
Matthew 16:22). They are ambitious in a clumsy and crude
way (Mark 9:33–34). They are chauvinists toward foreign-
ers, women and children (John 4:27; Matthew 19:13). And
they are cowards who abandoned the one they loved at the
moment of his supreme crisis (Mark 14:50).

It is this stark portrayal of the disciples which also makes it difficult to believe yet another theory: That the apostles were brilliant liars who faked the resurrection and circulated the lie of the gospel thereafter in order to found a cult with Jesus as the titular object but themselves as the actual Big Cheeses. The notion of the apostles as early founders of a Jim Jones-style cult falls apart when we compare them with *real* liars and cult leaders. Compare them with Stalin, Hitler, Mao, Pol Pot, Jim Jones and the other tyrants and con artists and you notice something instantly. The apostles carefully and dogmatically incorporated into their official literature a stark record of their own failures!

Stalin seldom encouraged the Party faithful to meditate on his failures. Hitler did not encourage the German press to dwell on his betrayals of trust. Pol Pot, Mao, Jim Jones, and Charles Manson are not especially known for encouraging their followers to keep careful written and liturgical records of their sins and reserve a special spot on the calendar to contemplate, year in and year out, their colossal acts of cowardice, stupidity and failure. Yet on the apostles' own authority, a careful reiteration of their tremendous and glaring faults was made a part of the life of the whole Church from its inception. Thus, the betrayal of Christ by Peter, the ambitious squabbles, the craven cowardice and the stupid incomprehension of the disciples was dutifully recorded in the gospels and canonized as the very word of God by the people they converted.

Cunning liars would also ditch from the record Christ's last words: "My God, my God, why have you forsaken me?" (Matthew 27:46; Mark 15:34). It doesn't look good when your God figure says this sort of thing. Nor is it likely a clever liar trying to invent a deity would have Jesus say

"Why do you call me good? No one is good — except God alone" (Mark 10:18) or "No one knows about that day or hour, not even the angels in heaven, nor the Son, but only the Father" (Matthew 24:36) or "Who touched me?" (Luke 8:45). Nor would a clever liar write of his fake God figure "He could not do many miracles there, except lay hands on a few sick people and heal them" (Mark 6:5). Apparent confessions of imperfection, weakness and ignorance are bad advertising in the cult founding biz.

Yet the apostles (and, significantly, their devoted chroniclers such as Luke and Mark) never buff these rough edges off the story. They consistently act like honest witnesses.

And these honest witnesses say they saw Christ Risen after death. Risen. Not a hallucination or a ghost, for they gave him fish to eat and touched him (Luke 24:39–42). Risen. Not a bedraggled torture survivor who crawled out of the tomb, limped into town with pierced heart, hands and feet (and massive blood loss from a merciless scourging) and convinced them he was the Conqueror of Death. And these honest witnesses were willing to die for their Faith in the Risen Christ (and what is more, to maintain that Faith over a lifetime of separation, hardship and suffering).

So we return again to the question Jesus asked: "Who do you say that I am?" If these people were honest, healthy people and they say — in fact over *five hundred* of them say (1 Corinthians 15:6) — "We saw the Risen Christ", how are we to answer? Once again, all the answers but one look ever more preposterous, till we are forced back to the ultimatum voiced by C. S. Lewis in *Mere Christianity*:

A man who was merely a man and said the sort of things Jesus said would not be a great moral teacher. He would either be a lunatic — on a level with the man who says he is a poached egg — or else he would be the Devil of Hell. You must make your choice. Either this man was, and is, the Son of God: or else a madman or something worse. You can shut Him up for a fool, you can spit at Him and kill Him as a demon; or you can fall at His feet and call Him Lord and God. But let us not come with any patronizing nonsense about His being a great teacher. He has not left that open to us. He did not intend to.[11]

It was then, this Jesus, this "Son of the living God" whom Paul and the other apostles announced not only in Athens, but in every Jewish synagogue and Gentile watering hole around the Mediterranean. For in him, the God who is God not only of the Jews but of the Gentiles as well had at last fulfilled his covenants with the human race and re-vealed himself, not only as the glory of his people Israel, but as the light of revelation to the Gentiles (Luke 2:32). It was in this light of the true identity of Jesus of Nazareth as nothing less than the incarnate God of Israel that the Church he founded henceforth began to read the word bequeathed to it by Israel. And in so doing, they found, at long last, the key to unlocking its mysteries: the Word or Logos made flesh (John 1:14).

---

[11] C. S. Lewis, *Mere Christianity, The Case for Christianity, Christian Behaviour, and Beyond Personality — Anniversary Edition* (New York: Macmillan, 1981), p. 45.

5

The Sixth Covenant as the Key to Scripture

The Early Christian was very precisely a person carrying about a key, or what he said was a key. The whole Christian movement consisted in claiming to possess that key.

— G. K. Chesterton

"Think not," says Jesus in Matthew 5:17, "that I have come to abolish the law and the prophets; I have come not to abolish them but to fulfil them." If we are to understand what the sixth and final covenant was to accomplish and how it relates to the other five covenants we have briefly surveyed (as well as to all the rest of Scripture), we have to engrave these words on our minds and hearts. For the reality is, Jesus' entire purpose is to fulfil all that has gone before in the Old Testament. Henceforth, we are to see none other than him and his gospel as the key to unlocking the mysteries of the Old Testament, says the Church he founded.

But, of course, the question naturally arises: Why? After all, the Old Testament writers usually don't seem to have Jesus in mind at all when they write. How could they since it would be pretty hard for, say, Abraham to be puzzling about a Messiah a thousand years before the term began to be bandied about in Israelite culture. How can we speak of Jesus as a "fulfillment" of things written by people who seem to have no conscious knowledge of him?

To answer that, we must look at what Jesus actually did. What was his mission?

Not to Teach a New Ethic Primarily

Jesus taught ethics. Everybody knows that. The Sermon on the Mount is, among other things, a string of ethical teachings. Yet Jesus did not come mainly to teach a new ethic. The reason we know that is because we know what Jesus taught, and it was, in many cases, nothing new. He reiterated a great deal of what any Jew already knew from the law of Moses or, for that matter, what any Confucian knew from Confucius, as that we should Do the Right Thing. Occasionally, as we shall see, he sometimes elevated the old ethical standards to higher applications. Yet, in all this, he promulgated no radically new ethics, merely an old ethic more profoundly understood. More often than not, he came, as Samuel Johnson notes that all good teachers of ethics come, to remind more than to instruct. Similarly, he did not advocate some radical break with the creed of Moses. He, like Moses and the prophets, reiterated the basic belief of all Judaism that "the Lord is One" and that we were to worship God alone. Nothing new here either. And this was not what impressed (and enraged) the people around him. So what did?

Not Wonder-Working Primarily

Some people think that wonder-working was the main thrust of Jesus' mission. Any talk show host can teach ethics, but only God can do miracles. Therefore, since (as we have seen) Jesus is God, he must have primarily come to do miracles so people would believe that God exists and be good. This seems all the more reasonable given the reaction his wonders excited. People believed in him after he walked on the Sea of Galilee (Matthew 14:28–33). People wanted to destroy him after he cured a man with a withered hand (Matthew 12:9–14). There was no middle ground. People accused him of blasphemy or fell at his feet when he worked wonders. So it might appear that *this* is what the gospels regard as the unique mission of Christ. But a wider view reveals a different perspective. For ancient Judea was no stranger to wonder-workers of all sizes and shapes. To the naked eye, the difference between miracle and magic is not readily apparent if you know nothing of the wonder-worker. Simon Magus did all sorts of impressive things which, to the casual observer, looked indistinguishable from the miracles of Jesus (Acts 8:9–10). And the literature of the period is chock full of magic and miracles from various sources.[1] This, of course, is why the Pharisees made just this charge against Jesus — that he was a deceiver operating by either demonic or human trickery to achieve effects they themselves could not explain (Matthew 12:24–27).

---

[1] Everett Ferguson, *Backgrounds of Early Christianity*, *Second Edition* (Grand Rapids: Eerdmans, 1993) pp. 207–218.

Of course, on close examination, we find that the testimony for Jesus' miracles does, in fact, mark him off from the other wonder-workers of the day. His power is displayed quietly and often with a command to "tell no one" (Mark 1:44). It is not wreathed round with the elaborate devices of words and invocations customary to establish one's professional status as a wonder-worker. It is not showy or self-aggrandizing. And, most striking, his power works, not in obscure out-of-the-way places, but repeatedly, in public, with complete strangers, and without the benefit of elaborate preparations (Mark 5:21–34). But the miracles, though astounding, do not mark him off as unique by themselves, for he himself acknowledges what all his countrymen believe: that other people work wonders too. Thus, Jesus rebukes the Pharisees for claiming "It is only by Be-elzebul [Satan], the prince of demons, that this man casts out demons" (Matthew 12:24). But note how he rebukes them. He appeals to the fact that the Pharisees' *own disciples* cast out devils too:

> [I]f I cast out demons by Be-elzebul, by whom do your sons cast them out? Therefore they shall be your judges. (Matthew 12:27)

So he himself makes clear he is not unique as a wonder-worker and it is not this, by itself, that sets his mission apart from all others. What does set his mission apart is, rather, the fact that God was giving him the miraculous power to do these things even when he was "blasphemously" making claims to deity. That is why Jesus continued:

> But if it is by the Spirit of God that I cast out demons, then the kingdom of God has come upon you. (Matthew 12:28)

In short, prophets like Elijah and exorcists in Jesus' own day could do wonders by the power of God just as he could. But only he claimed that the miracles were done by his *own* divine power and were an illustration of that power. The wonders, in other words, were not his main mission, according to Christ, they were the *signs* pointing to the main mission, just as a road sign points to a destination.

So, for instance, the gospels all recount the miracle of the multiplication of the loaves and fishes (see, for instance, John 6), but not because they want us to see a cool special effect for its own sake. Indeed, Jesus is specifically recorded as rebuking people for *seeing* signs but not *reading* them. He tells them: "Truly, truly, I say to you, you seek me, not because you saw signs, but because you ate your fill of the loaves" (John 6:26). In short, he rebukes them for seeing only a lot of bread in the miracle, but not seeing what the bread *means* — that he himself is the "bread of life" (John 6:35). Jesus (and the gospel writers) make it clear that this miracle (which happened near the time of the Passover) both recalls the manna given Israel as they wandered in the desert with Moses (Exodus 16) *and* is a foretaste of the bread Jesus will offer at another Passover supper a year hence: at the Last Supper when he will institute the Eucharist on the eve of his death and say, "This is my body" (Matthew 26:26; Mark 14:22; Luke 22:19; 1 Corinthians 11:24). And this pattern of a miraculous sign as a sort of finger pointing to the crucifixion and resurrection and its healing effects is repeated many times in the gospels. Jesus and the gospel writers urge us not to sniff like poodles at the pointing finger but rather to raise our eyes to behold what the finger is pointing at. When we do, we find that the *main* thing Jesus came to do was this:

Jesus Came to Die and Rise from the Dead "For the Life of the World"

Take a look at the gospels. If the mission of Christ was to work enough miracles that somebody would believe in him, then Matthew would have ended at chapter 16, for in that chapter, as we have seen, Peter confessed faith in him as Christ and Son of the living God. But that was not the main thing Jesus came to do. The main thing he came to do was summed up by the very next thing he told Peter and the apostles:

> From that time Jesus began to show his disciples that he must go to Jerusalem and suffer many things from the elders and chief priests and scribes, and be killed, and on the third day be raised. (Matthew 16:21)

That is what Jesus came to do. And that is what the gospels are focused on. This is why, when you think about it, each of the gospels skims over the entire life of Jesus with extraordinary compression of material. We get a few collections of sayings, the burden of which is that Jesus is giving us a new life and a new way of living based on his authority and power as God Incarnate.[2] We also get a few

---

[2] And so, for instance, Jesus declares "You have heard that it was said (by Moses) to believe or do X, but *I* say to believe or do Y" (see Matthew 5:21–44, for instance). In so speaking, Jesus claims the divine authority to alter, interpret, and amend the law God gave to Moses.

accounts of signs worked by him, every one of which signals something about Jesus or his ultimate mission to die, rise, and thereby somehow heal humanity. Then all four gospels settle down to devote about a quarter of their ink to talking about one week — the final week — of Jesus' life. Even that week is treated with relative lightness compared to the white hot focus fixed on what amounts to about a 72-hour period: the period from the Last Supper on Thursday night until the resurrection on Sunday. The fact that a writer focuses such enormous attention on such a narrow time span tells us quite clearly that this is the key to understanding his hero. The fact that not just one writer but all four do this tells us that the apostolic Tradition they are writing down is, as a whole, centered on the crucifixion and resurrection of Christ, rather than on the Sermon on the Mount or Christmas or walking on water, as the main point of the story of Christ. This is where the center of gravity is. This is Christ's mission.

Given this, let us then briefly survey again the covenants we have looked at previously and see some of the ways in which the revelation of God in the person and work of Jesus Christ throws the covenants of the Old Testament into new light, as well as the way in which these covenants help us to understand Christ more deeply.

The Covenant with Adam in Light of Christ

The connection between Christ and Adam is made early and explicit in the writings of the New Testament. The first mention of it shows up in the writings of Paul, which are the earliest apostolic writings we have.[3] Paul refers to Jesus as "the last Adam" (1 Corinthians 15:45) or as a sort of counterpart and contrast to the first Adam (Romans 5). The last Adam, in Paul's writings, mends what the first Adam destroyed by sin. And other New Testament writers note the same pattern. Thus, where the first Adam brings death to the race through the Tree of the Knowledge of Good and Evil, the last Adam brings life to the race through the Tree of the Cross. Where Adam succumbed to the devil in the Garden of Eden, Jesus fought and beat the devil in the Garden of Gethsemane. And where the first Adam was from the earth the last Adam is from heaven (1 Corinthians 15:47).

Moreover, Jesus not only mends what Adam damaged, he blesses what, in the first Adam, was good. And so, for instance, the New Testament insists that Jesus did not shed his humanity and dissolve back into pure spiritual deity at his resurrection. Jesus, though God, remains human, albeit glorified. Moreover, those who believe in him are promised the same destiny of glory. And so Paul promises the Romans, not that they will spend eternity with Christ as wispy bodiless spooks, but that "If the Spirit of him who raised

---

[3] The books of the New Testament are not arranged chronologically. The gospels were actually composed later than most of the epistles, and for an obvious reason: the epistles are written to help the new and struggling Church in its day-to-day practice and faith as it encountered the hurly-burly of life. The gospels were written later because the generation which witnessed the life of Christ realized that Jesus was not returning as soon as they had hoped and so set down its testimony for the sake of its descendants. In the same way, people today write letters long before they write memoirs.

Jesus from the dead dwells in you, he who raised Christ Jesus from the dead will *give life to your mortal bodies also* through his Spirit which dwells in you" (Romans 8:11). In short, it is the sin — not the humanness — of the first Adam that the last Adam comes to cure. All that is truly human in Adam, including his bodily existence, will be preserved and glorified in Christ.

Jesus himself makes this same point of identification with Adam by referring to himself constantly as the "Son of Man." That is, he is claiming to somehow mysteriously sum up in himself all humanity. He regards an act of charity toward any person as an act of charity toward himself. Conversely, he sees any act of injustice toward any person as an act of injustice toward himself. That is, he speaks of himself as though he *is* Humanity. This is the substance of the parable of the sheep and goats in Matthew 25. It is also the assumption that underlies every act of forgiveness he granted to strangers who could not possibly have sinned against him personally.

In addition to proclaiming Jesus a kind of second Adam, the Church sees something else: a second Eve. This insight takes several forms. The Church itself, for instance, is referred to repeatedly as the Bride of Christ (Ephesians 5; Revelation 22:17). But in addition, the gospels repeatedly tend to focus on one person — Mary — as a kind of icon of the Bride. And so, for instance, when John wishes to show us the first and archetypal miracle of Christ he shows Christ present at — where else? — a wedding. And who is it that pleads for Messiah to pour out that sign of messianic bounty which is wine?[4] Mary who, years before, had be-

---

[4] See, for example, Isaiah 25:6–8, which curiously associates bountiful

come the bride of God by saying, "Be it unto me according to thy will."

And, as Mary is the icon of the Bride of the second Adam, so also, like Eve, she is shown (particularly in the gospel of John) as the Mother of the children of the second Adam. And so John carefully preserves this scene from the crucifixion:

> [S]tanding by the cross of Jesus were his mother, and his mother's sister, Mary the wife of Clopas, and Mary Magdalene. When Jesus saw his mother, and the disciple whom he loved standing near, he said to his mother, "Woman, behold, your son!" Then he said to the disciple, "Behold, your mother!" And from that hour the disciple took her to his own home. (John 19:25–27)

John is not simply interested in chatting about first-century Palestinian domestic arrangements for widows. As with all the details from his gospel, this scene also is written down for a theological purpose: "that you may believe that Jesus is the Christ, the Son of God, and that believing you may have life in his name" (John 20:31). And the purpose is pretty clear here. Just as Jesus is the parallel of Adam, so Mary is the parallel of Eve (whose name means "mother of the living"). This is why Irenaeus, who was a disciple of

---

wine with the destruction of death: "On this mountain the LORD of hosts will make for all peoples a feast of fat things, a feast of wine on the lees, of fat things full of marrow, of wine on the lees well refined. And he will destroy on this mountain the covering that is cast over all peoples, the veil that is spread over all nations. He will swallow up death for ever, and the Lord GOD will wipe away tears from all faces, and the reproach of his people he will take away from all the earth; for the LORD has spoken."

Polycarp, who had heard the Apostle John with his own
ears, tells us that Mary

> being obedient, was made the cause of salvation for her-
> self and for the whole human race. . . . Thus, the knot of
> Eve's disobedience was loosed by the obedience of Mary.
> What the virgin Eve had bound in unbelief, the Virgin
> Mary loosed through faith.[5]

In short, as the Fall was a social sin that involved both
man and woman, so the redemption is social as well. As
Jesus is the second Adam for the writers of the New Testament, so Mary is linked with Eve as the one who was
graced to undo woman's contribution to the Fall. For as
Irenaeus notes, she chose the opposite of Eve: She chose to
say yes to God. In so doing, Mary became the true "Mother
of all the living" in union with the second Adam, in contrast to Eve who became the Mother of all the dying in
union with the first Adam.

John hammers home this linkage between the second
Adam and his "Bride" in his account of the crucifixion.
For at the very climax of the story, a curious thing happens
which John obviously regards as extremely important. He
writes:

> [O]ne of the soldiers pierced his side with a spear, and
> at once there came out blood and water. He who saw it
> has borne witness — his testimony is true, and he knows
> that he tells the truth — that you also may believe. (John
> 19:34–35)

Why does John interrupt the narrative of his gospel here,
of all places, to make sure we believe that blood and wa-

---

[5] Irenaeus, *Adversus Haereses*, 3, 22, 4.

ter gushed from Jesus' side? Is he really interested in the anatomical details of pericardial rupture? No. He is interested in pointing out the *meaning* of this event, which he saw with his own eyes: namely, that the Church, the Bride of the second Adam, is born from Jesus' side in the waters of baptism just as the first Eve was made from the side of the first Adam. For John, there is a clear and obvious connection between "the spirit, the water, and the blood" (John 5:8). It is "of water and the Spirit" flowing from the bleeding side of Jesus, that Christ cleansed the Bride "by the washing of water with the word, that he might present the Church to himself in splendor, without spot or wrinkle or any such thing, that she might be holy and without blemish" (Ephesians 5:26–27). The creation of the second Eve parallels the creation of the first.

And that is because Christ parallels Adam in another way. He is a Priest King — *the* Priest King — set over the garden of Creation to fulfill what Adam failed to fulfill. He undoes the curse. And so where Adam's work of ruling over creation is doomed to never-ending futility and his body to death, Christ says of his work at the very last, "It is finished!" (John 19:30) and his body is raised to life. Where Adam refused to offer himself, Christ offered himself utterly as both priest and victim (Hebrews 9:11–14). And where Adam followed his bride down to destruction, the second Adam pulls his Bride up from destruction by his death and resurrection so that she may "bear much fruit" that will abide to the glory of God the Father (John 15:8). In other words, Jesus heals the damage to the primal human mission of marriage, fruitfulness, rule, work, and worship wrought upon us when the serpent struck our heel. In fulfillment of God's promise to Eve, the "seed of the woman" at long last finally and definitively crushes the serpent's head. And he does so by the thing hinted at in Genesis when God clothed his fallen children with the skins of animals: his own bloody death.

The Covenant with Noah in Light of Christ

The New Testament sees similar connections being made in the story of Noah. As has already been noted, both the covenants with Adam and Noah summarize the situation of Gentile humanity before the coming of Christ: created in God's image (and therefore equal in dignity with the Chosen People), fallen (like the Chosen People), but hitherto not privy to the special revelation entrusted to Israel. In the covenant with Noah, we have a picture of a human race endowed with a basic moral sense of frontier justice ("[w]hoever sheds the blood of man, by man shall his blood be shed; for God made man in his own image" [Genesis 9:6]), with a basic recollection of humanity's primal mission in Adam ("And you, be fruitful and multiply, bring forth abundantly on the earth and multiply in it" [Genesis 9:7]), and with a basic sense of the obligation to render worship to God ("Then Noah built an altar to the LORD, and took of every clean animal and of every clean bird, and offered burnt offerings on the altar" [Genesis 8:20]). Beyond that however, special revelation has not been granted. As the psalmist observes:

> He declares his word to Jacob,
> his statutes and ordinances to Israel.
> He has not dealt thus with any other nation;
> they do not know his ordinances. (Psalm 147:19–20)

So, as we have seen, in the absence of special revelation the Gentiles have been left to providentially feel their way toward God. They have, till the advent of Christ, remained "alienated from the commonwealth of Israel, and strangers to the covenants of promise" (Ephesians 2:12).

This alienation has, as we noted, led to the universal blunder of idolatry. That blunder is rooted not only in an intellectual mistake but in a sinful moral choice. At some level, sooner or later, the human soul recognizes that attractive creatures such as money, sex, power, or golden calves (which symbolize all three), are nonetheless not what life is about. If one persists in worshipping them when their inadequacy becomes plain rather than, like Socrates, casting about for something more, one has not merely made a "mistake." One has committed a sin against the truth. And that is a sin against God, even if you don't happen to know his name.

Moreover, it is an even worse sin if you *do* happen to know his name, as Israel did. Thus, the New Testament writers are, for understandable reasons, particularly moved to see in the story of Noah the theme of judgment against persistent unbelief. The gospels repeatedly record Jesus warning his hearers to be ready for his Second Coming at the end of the world in these terms:

> As were the days of Noah, so will be the coming of the Son of man. For as in those days before the flood they were eating and drinking, marrying and giving in marriage, until the day when Noah entered the ark, and they did not know until the flood came and swept them all away, so will be the coming of the Son of man. (Matthew 24:37–39)

But though the theme of judgment is clearly present, even more clear is the New Testament's interest in the possibility and promise of salvation. For the sixth covenant extends not to a couple, not to a family, not to a tribe, not to a nation, and not to a kingdom, but to the whole world, including the Gentiles. And so Peter makes this startling connection between the flood of Noah and the waters of baptism:

> For Christ also died for sins once for all, the righteous for the unrighteous, that he might bring us to God, being put to death in the flesh but made alive in the spirit; in which he went and preached to the spirits in prison, who formerly did not obey, when God's patience waited in the days of Noah, during the building of the ark, in which a few, that is, eight persons, were saved through water. Baptism, which corresponds to this, now saves you, not as a removal of dirt from the body but as an appeal to God for a clear conscience, through the resurrection of Jesus Christ, who has gone into heaven and is at the right hand of God, with angels, authorities, and powers subject to him. (1 Peter 3:18–22)

The waters no longer destroy humanity; they give life. The ark is no longer a boat with room enough for eight. It is now the Church of Christ and it encompasses not only the Jews but the long-alienated Gentiles as well. As St. Paul says:

> So then you are no longer strangers and sojourners, but you are fellow citizens with the saints and members of the household of God, built upon the foundation of the apostles and prophets, Christ Jesus himself being the cornerstone, in whom the whole structure is joined together and grows into a holy temple in the Lord; in whom you

also are built into it for a dwelling place of God in the Spirit. (Ephesians 2:19–22)

Moreover, as the waters of the Flood are transformed by the waters of baptism that poured from the side of Christ, so the prohibition against eating blood is transformed by the blood that poured from the side of Christ. As you recall, Noah was given the strange warning by God "[Y]ou shall not eat flesh with its life, that is, its blood" (Genesis 9:4) because, in the words of Deuteronomy 12:23, "the blood is the life." The intention of this strange command is to head us off from the idea (still preserved in many tribal cultures) that we could or should attempt to acquire our life from any creature. In essence, the prohibition against eating blood means, "Do not seek the majesty of the lion by eating the blood of the lion. Do not seek the speed of the ostrich by eating the blood of the ostrich. Do not seek the strength of the ox by eating the blood of the ox. Give the life back to God and seek your life from him alone, O man." In short, the command is meant to prevent a kind of idolatry by reminding us of our complete dependence on God and not on any creature. For the same reason, of course, Israel is forbidden to worship any man.

But when God himself becomes a flesh and blood man in Christ Jesus, everything is different and a second meaning to the commandment appears. What was forbidden *before* the Incarnation is now commanded in one unique situation *after* it. Before the Incarnation, no man could be worshipped; after it, the man Christ Jesus *must* be worshipped because he is God. Likewise, before the Incarnation, the blood of no mere creature may be eaten; after it, the blood of the Word made flesh and blood *must* be eaten.

Why? Because the blood is the life and Jesus — the Way, the Truth and the *Life* (John 14:6) — tells us, "Truly, truly, I say to you, unless you eat the flesh of the Son of man and drink his blood, *you have no life in you*; he who eats my flesh and drinks my blood has eternal life" (John 6:53–54).

As with the covenant with Adam, the covenant with Noah is also completed and fulfilled by the sixth covenant in Christ. This is why Revelation 4:3 shows us the throne of God in heaven surrounded by the central sign of the covenant with Noah: a rainbow.

This brings us back to the last of the three promises given to Abraham and the complaint mentioned in Chapter 3 of the supposed 'tribalism' God displayed in choosing that ancient chieftain out of all the nations of the earth. For an idolatrous humanity which was increasingly living in its imagination as the means to finding God did not need more imaginary gods, it needed the real one. A race of dreamers did not need more dreams. It needed to wake up. And so it was necessary that, at some point or other, real revelation from the real God should crystallize out of the hints and guesses of Gentile mythic imagination into the more prosaic workaday world of history. It was necessary that guesses be supplanted by revelation, theories by truth, and myth by fact. It was necessary that the Messiah of the sixth covenant — the Word made flesh — come from *somewhere*, not from everywhere or nowhere. And so, it was necessary that God choose a particular man, race, nation, and tribe as the forebears of that Man. *That* is why the story is condensed down to a particular family: Abraham's family. God's revelation to the human race did not get "exclusive" with Abraham. It got focused. And it got focused on the Chosen People for the sake of the unchosen.

The Covenant with Abraham in Light of Christ

"By you," says God to Abraham, "all the families of the earth shall bless themselves" (Genesis 12:3). This is the promise still unfulfilled at the close of the Old Testament, and this is the promise which St. Paul takes special care to note in Galatians 3:6–9:

> Abraham "believed God, and it was reckoned to him as righteousness." So you see that it is men of faith who are the sons of Abraham. And the scripture, foreseeing that God would justify the Gentiles by faith, preached the gospel beforehand to Abraham, saying, "In you shall all the nations be blessed." So then, those who are men of faith are blessed with Abraham who had faith.

How are all the nations blessed through Abraham? "By faith," says Paul. What does that mean? It means, says Paul, that we enter into the life of God's grace not by racking up brownie points and putting God in our debt, but by receiving his life poured out for us in the sacrificial death and resurrection of his Son. Abraham's act of believing God, notes Paul, was reckoned to him as righteousness *before*, not after, he was circumcised (Romans 4:10). Therefore, says Paul, Abraham is "father of all who believe without being circumcised and who thus have righteousness reckoned to them, and likewise the father of the circumcised who are not merely circumcised but also follow the example of the faith which our father Abraham had before he was circumcised" (Romans 4:11–12). This, says Paul, is one of the central aspects of "the mystery of Christ, which was not made known to the sons of men in other generations as it has now been revealed to his holy apostles and prophets by the Spirit; that is, how the Gentiles are fellow heirs, members of the same body, and partakers of the promise in Christ Jesus through the gospel." (Ephesians 3:4–6)

Long ago, says the writer to the Hebrews, "Abraham, when he was tested, offered up Isaac, and he who had received the promises was ready to offer up his only son, of whom it was said, 'Through Isaac shall your descendants be named.' He considered that God was able to raise men even from the dead; hence, figuratively speaking, he did receive him back" (Hebrews 11:17–19). Now, in strict fact, Abraham's descendants, to this very day, include not only the descendants of Isaac, but of Ishmael as well. Did God then abandon Ishmael? By no means. We know from Genesis that Ishmael did quite well. What then does God mean? He means that the messianic line will be traced through Isaac, not Ishmael. The Messiah will have a particular set of fingerprints and a particular genealogy, like all real people. Moreover, his forbear Isaac shall stand as the great sign of the coming sixth covenant, because what Abraham was asked to perform as a kind of figure or shadow, God himself did in all reality: he offered his Son, his only Son, whom he loved. And through him everyone, children of Isaac *and* Ishmael, can become sons and daughters of God by faith — the faith of Abraham. Through him all the nations of the earth are blessed.

But not immediately.

The Covenant with Moses in Light of Christ

As we have already seen, the covenant with Moses comes first. Why?

The paradoxical answer, given through St. Paul, is essentially this: it comes to show that it could not be kept. As Paul writes:

> No human being will be justified in his sight by works of the law, since through the law comes knowledge of sin. But now the righteousness of God has been manifested apart from law, although the law and the prophets bear witness to it, the righteousness of God through faith in Jesus Christ for all who believe. For there is no distinction; since all have sinned and fall short of the glory of God, they are justified by his grace as a gift, through the redemption which is in Christ Jesus, whom God put forward as an expiation by his blood, to be received by faith. (Romans 3:20–25)

The paradoxical role the Mosaic covenant plays in God's plan to heal the world from the fall of Adam turns out to be the paradox of an x-ray machine. It is a tool used in the healing process, but it is not a tool that can heal. If you want to know where a bone is broken, you need an x-ray machine. But if you want to heal the broken bone, increasing the dose of radiation will not do the trick. So here. The law can x-ray the broken soul of the fallen children of Adam and Eve, but it cannot heal it. The covenant with Moses, by its very nature, cannot be the last word in the promise of worldwide blessing given to Abraham for the very simple reason that the law can't bless. It was, by nature, provisional and impermanent. This is why "the law and the prophets bear witness" to the Divine Physician and to our need for his saving help. According to Paul, if we make the mistake of imagining the law and prophets are the main attraction or the central story of Scripture, we make the same mistake as a person who confuses an x-ray machine with healing, a sign post with a destination, or a diagnosis with a treatment.

Jesus himself speaks of the same paradox when he declares, "You search the scriptures, because you think that in them you have eternal life; and it is they that bear witness to me" (John 5:39). "The scriptures" for Jesus' audience means primarily the law and the prophets, and Jesus is here saying exactly the same thing as Paul. Namely, that the law can only tell us what's wrong with us. It cannot save us for it cannot change us. Only God can. But to do that, he must, as he promised to do through the prophet Jeremiah, inaugurate a new covenant — the sixth covenant consisting of a new creed, code, and cult. And, sure enough, this is what Jesus does.

The credal aspect of the sixth covenant is summarized nicely in Matthew 28:19–20:

> Go therefore and make disciples of all nations, baptizing them in the name of the Father and of the Son and of the Holy Spirit, teaching them to observe all that I have commanded you; and lo, I am with you always, to the close of the age.

That is, we must believe not only that God is one (as the Old Testament commands), we must believe that the oneness of God is the Trinitarian oneness of love between the three persons of the Blessed Trinity — a love that encompasses and empowers Christ's Church. From this embryonic credal statement will flow all the subsequent creeds of the Church.

Similarly, the code of Moses is completed and fulfilled by the new law of love in Christ. "Completed" because Jesus is, as we have seen, not a quack vending a radical new system of ethics but is rather the very God who spoke to Moses on Mt. Sinai and who has now come to complete the work he began there. Therefore, Jesus quotes Deuteronomy, one of the books his Spirit inspired:

> "You shall love the Lord your God with all your heart, and with all your soul, and with all your mind." This is the great and first commandment. And a second is like it, "You shall love your neighbor as yourself." On these two commandments depend all the law and the prophets. (Matthew 22:37–40)

Yet Jesus also makes these commands new. For in making the second one "like" the first one he emphasizes in a profound new way the link between love of God and love of neighbor. And he re-emphasizes that link in many ways ranging from his command to love enemies to his demand for unlimited forgiveness for all who hurt us. It is the paradox of this old-yet-new quality of the new law of Christ that John is getting at when he writes

> Beloved, I am writing you no new commandment, but an old commandment which you had from the beginning; the old commandment is the word which you have heard. Yet I am writing you a new commandment, which is true in him and in you, because the darkness is passing away and the true light is already shining. He who says he is in the light and hates his brother is in the darkness still. He who loves his brother abides in the light, and in it there is no cause for stumbling. (1 John 2:7–10)

Finally, the new covenant, like the old, necessarily involves sacrifice: the sacrifice, not of an animal, but of Jesus himself, at once high priest and "Lamb of God, who takes away the sin of the world" (Hebrews 8; John 1:29). That sacrifice is, of course, the passion and resurrection of Jesus which took place 2,000 years ago in Jerusalem. But, as Paul tells the Corinthians, the Church has an ongoing mystical and miraculous access to that event in the present tense: the Eucharist. That is why he tells the Corinthians, "The cup of blessing which we bless, is it not a participation in the blood of Christ? The bread which we break, is it not a participation in the body of Christ? Because there is one bread, we who are many are one body, for we all partake of the one bread." (1 Corinthians 10:16–17). And Paul gets this idea from Jesus Christ himself who, during the Passover seder he celebrated on the night he was betrayed

> took bread, and when he had given thanks he broke it and gave it to them, saying, "This is my body which is given for you. Do this in remembrance of me." And likewise the cup after supper, saying, "This cup which is poured out for you is the new covenant in my blood." (Luke 22:19–20)

This leads to a further paradox. On one hand, the sixth covenant means that anybody at all can become a member of the covenant people by imitating the faith of Abraham. On the other hand, it emphatically does not mean that anyone can be a member of the covenant people by having faith in anything at all. The covenant comes to us through the death and resurrection of one specific person: Jesus Christ and nobody else. And Jesus Christ, being a real human being and not some myth like Osiris, has a real lineage which the Scriptures are at pains to trace. Two gospels (Matthew and Luke) do it and Paul frequently alludes to Jesus' heritage as "son of David" and therefore of the lineage of Abraham, Isaac, and Jacob. Likewise John, in his book of Revelation, refers to Jesus as the "Lion of the tribe of Judah", not of the tribe of Asher, Dan, or Benjamin (Revelation 5:5). But here's the rub: Judah was not a priestly tribe. Under the Mosaic covenant, priesthood fell to the tribe of Levi. How then could a serious Jew speak of Jesus as "priest and victim" as we have noted above since he is not a Levite?

The Covenant with David in Light of Christ

The answer to this riddle is already hinted at in the story of Abraham, and even more in the story of David. Recall the mysterious figure of Melchizedek, the priest king of Salem. Now the priestly tribe responsible for the sacrificial cult *under Mosaic law* is the Levites. But the Mosaic law came long after Abraham. Levites are descendants of Levi, one of the twelve sons of Jacob. Jacob's great-grandfather is Abraham, and Abraham is obviously understood to be greater than Jacob, let alone Levi. And yet, as we have seen, out of nowhere appears the mysterious figure of Melchizedek, who offers priestly sacrifice and to whom Abraham pays the tithe. And this can only mean that Abraham regards Melchizedek as even greater than he is. In short, there is hinted at in the Old Testament, the possibility of a priesthood far greater than the Levitical priesthood.

This hint gets louder when, in Psalm 110 — a psalm widely recognized in first century Judaism as messianic — the psalmist, universally understood to be David in Jesus' day, declares

The LORD says to my lord:
"Sit at my right hand,
    till I make your enemies your footstool."
The LORD sends forth from Zion your mighty scepter.
    Rule in the midst of your foes!
Your people will offer themselves freely
    on the day you lead your host upon the holy mountains.
From the womb of the morning like dew
    your youth will come to you.
The LORD has sworn and will not change his mind,
"You are a priest for ever after the order of Melchizedek."
(Psalm 110:1–4)

This psalm, in light of the revelation of the sixth covenant, presented traditional Palestinian messianic belief with
a problem. That problem was highlighted by Jesus himself:

> Now while the Pharisees were gathered together, Jesus
> asked them a question, saying, "What do you think of the
> Christ? Whose son is he?" They said to him, "The son
> of David." He said to them, "How is it then that David,
> inspired by the Spirit, calls him Lord, saying, 'The Lord
> said to my Lord, Sit at my right hand, till I put thy ene-
> mies under thy feet'? If David thus calls him Lord, how
> is he his son?" (Matthew 22:41–45)

In a nutshell, Jesus is asking, "Just who is the Messiah that David himself should call him Lord?" He is,
in fact, making a subtle but unmistakable hint that the
Messiah, the "priest forever" after the order of none other
than Melchizedek described by Psalm 110, is not simply a
conquering king. Moreover, Messiah is no mere Levitical
priest. He is a priest king like Melchizedek greater than
David, greater than Levi, greater than Moses, greater than
even Abraham.

Just how much greater Jesus makes clear when he re-marks:

> Your father Abraham rejoiced that he was to see my day; he saw it and was glad." The Jews then said to him, "You are not yet fifty years old, and have you seen Abraham?" Jesus said to them, "Truly, truly, I say to you, before Abraham was, I am." (John 8:56–58)

"I AM" is more than merely a claim to eternal existence (though that alone ought to take our breath away). "I AM" is the very name of God in the Hebrew tongue. Jesus is claiming to be that very God who appeared to Moses in the burning bush in Exodus 3, who inaugurated the covenant with Moses on Mt. Sinai in the wilderness, and who called Abram out of Ur of the Chaldeans. It is because of this that the earliest Jewish Christians ultimately saw the reality that the sixth covenant fulfilled all that the Levitical sacrificial system was pointing to. This is why the writer to the Hebrews tells us:

> Now if perfection had been attainable through the Levitical priesthood (for under it the people received the law), what further need would there have been for another priest to arise after the order of Melchizedek, rather than one named after the order of Aaron? For when there is a change in the priesthood, there is necessarily a change in the law as well. For the one of whom these things are spoken belonged to another tribe, from which no one has ever served at the altar. For it is evident that our Lord was descended from Judah, and in connection with that tribe Moses said nothing about priests.
>
> This becomes even more evident when another priest arises in the likeness of Melchizedek, who has become a

priest, not according to a legal requirement concerning bodily descent but by the power of an indestructible life. For it is witnessed of him, "Thou art a priest for ever, after the order of Melchizedek." On the one hand, a former commandment is set aside because of its weakness and uselessness (for the law made nothing perfect); on the other hand, a better hope is introduced, through which we draw near to God. (Hebrews 7:11–19)

Here, in sum, is the way the sixth covenant illuminates the covenant with David. In light of Christ, the apostles at last came to see the mysterious point of the law that had to be kept yet could not be kept. They saw that "the law made nothing perfect." They saw that there is another priesthood, and therefore another law, which God himself had established "by the power of an indestructible life." And David, by the power of the Holy Spirit, seems to have curiously intuited the same thing. For, as we saw, he sought to re-enact the priest king role of Melchizedek. Wearing the priestly ephod and offering priestly sacrifice, he gave bread and wine as Melchizedek once did and sought to build God a temple. But God did not permit it. For David was not Messiah. He could, for a season, play the role of a priest king, but he could not really fill the shoes. That task can only be accomplished by the "Son of David" whom God said would "build his house" and whom Psalm 110 calls "my Lord." And David himself bore tragic witness to his inadequacy by his sin with Bathsheba. As Paul says of the Mosaic covenant, so the same might be said of David's odd dalliance with the priesthood of Melchizedek: he was "only a shadow of what is to come; but the substance belongs to Christ" (Colossians 2:17). Like the law of Moses, the covenant with David was a great and holy image and foreshadow, but it could not of itself make anyone holy, just or good. It could only refer us to the one who can: Jesus Christ, God incarnate, crucified and risen, who took on the flesh of Adam for all the children of Noah and Abraham and fulfilled the law of Moses as the long-awaited son of David.

It is to this God-Man that the Church he founded is continually pointing in the aftermath of these events. All the actions it will perform subsequent to this mystery of death and resurrection will hark back to and mysteriously participate in it. Thus, baptism is described this way:

> Do you not know that all of us who have been baptized into Christ Jesus were baptized into his death? We were buried therefore with him by baptism into death, so that as Christ was raised from the dead by the glory of the Father, we too might walk in newness of life. For if we have been united with him in a death like his, we shall certainly be united with him in a resurrection like his. (Romans 6:3–5)

Similarly, the oils of anointing will link healing with the forgiveness of sins bought "by his blood" (James 5:16; Ephesians 1:7), marriage is seen as a participation in the mystical union of Christ with his Bride the Church, whom he "gave himself up for" to death (Ephesians 5:25), and the life, teaching and worship celebrated by the Church is not seen to be a collection of customs fadged up willy-nilly by "followers" but is, instead, seen to be the unified action of "the body of Christ" in union with the Head, its risen Lord. This is precisely why Paul writes

> There is one body and one Spirit, just as you were called to the one hope that belongs to your call, one Lord, one

faith, one baptism, one God and Father of us all, who is
above all and through all and in all. But grace was given
to each of us according to the measure of Christ's gift.
. . . And his gifts were that some should be apostles, some
prophets, some evangelists, some pastors and teachers, to
equip the saints for the work of ministry, for building up
the body of Christ, until we all attain to the unity of the
faith and of the knowledge of the Son of God, to mature
manhood, to the measure of the stature of the fulness of
Christ; so that we may no longer be children, tossed to
and fro and carried about with every wind of doctrine, by
the cunning of men, by their craftiness in deceitful wiles.
Rather, speaking the truth in love, we are to grow up in
every way into him who is the head, into Christ, from
whom the whole body, joined and knit together by every
joint with which it is supplied, when each part is working
properly, makes bodily growth and upbuilds itself in love.
(Ephesians 4:4–7; 11–16)

This means vastly more than the proposition that Jesus
revealed some odorless, tasteless, "invisible" truth or set
of ideas. It means that a visible communion of sinners in
need of salvation will for all future time — despite their
sins, foibles, and follies — be linked unbreakably to the
God-Man's own authority and power as they submit to the
slow, painful, and awkward process of being changed into
a communion of saints. That is why Jesus tells the apostles, "He who hears you hears me, and he who rejects you
rejects me, and he who rejects me rejects him who sent
me" (Luke 10:16). And this, in turn, is why the apostles
themselves delegate successors (such as Timothy, Titus, and
the "elders" mentioned in Acts 14:23 and 15:6) to conserve
that life, teaching, and worship and hand it down to pos-

terity. The apostles and the Church they founded look at the command of the risen Christ to bear the life of the Father, Son, and Holy Spirit to the whole world (Matthew 28:16–20) and take seriously his promise that, from here to "the end of the age" he will be with the Church, guiding it into all truth by his Spirit (John 16:13). Therefore, since the Church's common life, teaching and worship spring from the central mystery of the death and resurrection of the Messiah as revealed through the apostles he sent out, the early Christians receive the whole of the apostolic Tradition they deliver, "whether by word-of-mouth or by letter" (2 Thessalonians 2:15).

This means that, from the apostolic age on, revelation will reflect the Trinitarian nature of the now-fully-revealed God who is Father, Son, and Holy Spirit. That is, revelation will be *symphonic*, not monotone. Rather than simply handing us a book called the Bible, Jesus hands us a Spirit-filled Body of Christ governed by apostolic successors (called "bishops") in union with a successor of Peter. This Body preserves its apostolic Tradition in both written and unwritten form. Every book in the New Testament is either a recounting of the events surrounding that unthinkably awesome event (as, for instance, in the Gospels and Acts), what that event means for us who live in its illumination (as in the Epistles), or where that event will ultimately lead us if we let it (as in Revelation). But the Bible does not stand alone. It lives in the context of the community created by Christ: the Body of Christ in union with the bishops and Pope in succession from the apostles.

It cannot be stressed enough that the written and unwritten Tradition handed down and conserved by this apostolic Church cannot be added to yet, paradoxically, constantly develops. It cannot be added to because there is nothing more to add. God has spoken his complete Word in the Word made flesh. There is nothing more God has to say.

But there's plenty more for us to understand, and God's Spirit is there to help the Church understand it. Not surprisingly then, in the pages of the New Testament itself we find Christians already attempting to penetrate more deeply into the mystery of the Tradition the apostles hand down to them (as, for instance, when the Council of Jerusalem was obliged to wrestle with the Old Testament requirement of circumcision in Acts 15). That Council, like all subsequent Catholic councils and doctrinal developments, added nothing new to the revelation given by Christ to his apostles. Rather, it simply came to understand more deeply the revelation he had already given. Thus, there is a real difference between "development of doctrine" (which the Church welcomes) and additional revelation (which the Church says is impossible from the death of the apostles until the return of Christ). It is the difference between a baby boy growing up to be a man with a beard and a baby boy growing up to be a man with extra noses and ears. The function of the bishops and Pope in succession from the apostles is to make sure the Church's Tradition *grows*, not mutates. As in Acts 2:42, the Church in union with the bishops and Pope will therefore devote itself to the apostles' teaching, to fellowship, to the breaking of bread and to the prayers. That is, by God's grace it conserves and develops the written and unwritten Tradition, the common life ("fellowship") and the common eucharistic, liturgical worship of the Church ("the breaking of bread and the prayers") — a life and worship that is essentially public and communal. This is necessary for the Church in the New Testament as for the Catholic Church today, because the common teaching, common life and common worship is *living* — like a mustard seed planted by Christ which has not ceased growing (Mark 4:30–32). No fully grown mustard plant looks like the seed, yet it is more, not less, mustardy than ever.

This leads us to the relationship of the New Testament with the Old and to the realization that Scripture not only may but *must* be understood as having more than one sense or meaning. For, as we have seen, the New Testament writers do not see the roots of the mustard plant merely extending back to the birth of Christ, as though he were an afterthought to all the history of Israel from which he sprang. Rather, they see Jesus and his mystical Body the Church as being in the Plan of God from the very start since he is God and was God from all eternity and he therefore orchestrated it all from "the foundation of the world" (John 1:1; Ephesians 1:4). This fact of Jesus' eternal divine existence from before all worlds is The Thing that throws a completely new light on the Old Testament and makes it as much a part of the Christian Bible as the New Testament. It is toward this God-Become-Man, risen from death to give the world new life, that *all* revelation has been pointing and straining since the beginning. It is he himself who is "the fulfillment of the Scriptures" as the apostles repeatedly say. It is of him, his death and resurrection, and its effects that all the Old Testament prophets have prophesied. It is toward him that all the events of the sacred history of Israel have been ordered, and all Creation — including Gentile creation — has groaned in the search for completion and fulfillment. Thus, it is not merely the signs worked by Christ's own hands during his earthly lifetime which are understood to point to him, it is Everything — and especially Scripture and all the signs of the Old Testament — that does so. The entire Old Testament in all its strange richness and variety is seen to be the written preparation for Christ while Christ is seen to throw a shocking and stark new light on the Hebrew Scripture. And so, the apostles teach, as St. Augustine observed, that God arranged for the New Testament to be hidden in the Old and the Old to be made manifest in the New. Therefore, the whole Bible, even the parts filled with bloodshed, weird prophecies, seemingly irrelevant census statistics, oddball miracles and cryptic images, is really about him.

Lest we imagine that this way of looking at Scripture is simply a feverish enthusiasm of the Middle Ages, we must note that Jesus himself — that is, God in human flesh and therefore the Author and Subject of all inspired Revelation — explicitly taught exactly the same thing on the very day he rose from the dead. Luke 24 tells the story of how he appeared to the disciples on the Emmaus Road and how they, in turn, rushed back to Jerusalem to tell the apostles, whereupon Jesus appeared to them and, to assure them he was real and not a ghost, ate a piece of fish in front of them and invited them to touch him to make sure they weren't hallucinating or something. When his bodily resurrection was fully established, he then told them:

> "These are my words which I spoke to you, while I was still with you, that everything written about me in the law of Moses and the prophets and the psalms must be fulfilled." Then he opened their minds to understand the scriptures, and said to them, *"Thus it is written, that the Christ should suffer and on the third day rise from the dead, and that repentance and forgiveness of sins should be preached in his name to all nations, beginning from Jerusalem."* (Luke 24:44–49)

In other words, the God-Man himself, not simply some medieval enthusiasts long after him, taught that the Old Testament was really about him, his death and resurrection, and the founding of the Church that would henceforth be his mystical body in the world. That is why Paul, following his Master, says to the Christians of Corinth that the passion and resurrection happened "in accordance with the Scriptures" (1 Corinthians 15:3–4) and why all the books of the New Testament speak continually of Jesus "fulfilling the Scriptures." Likewise, Paul insists that the Old Testament writings, in addition to whatever original audience the authors envisioned, were "written down for *our* instruction" (1 Corinthians 10:11). St. Augustine and the rest of the patristic and medieval Church, then, are simply reiterating what Jesus taught his disciples: namely, if you want to understand the Old Testament the very first thing you have to understand is that whatever the "letter" of a given text or book, it is the Holy Spirit of Christ that stands behind it (2 Corinthians 3:3–18) and that Spirit's inspiration of Scripture means that "no prophecy ever came by the impulse of man, but men moved by the Holy Spirit spoke from God" (2 Peter 1:20). Therefore, Jesus Christ, who is both God and Man, is the ultimate key to the Scriptures whose authors are both divine and human. And that key unlocks the Scripture to reveal both literal and other, more-than-literal senses, known as the allegorical, moral, and anagogical senses. In the following chapters, we will look more closely at these senses of Scripture to discover some of the ways in which they help us to delve more deeply into the biblical message.

PART II

The Four Senses
of Scripture

6

The Literal Sense of Scripture

I meant what I said and I said what I meant. . . . An elephant's faithful one hundred per cent!
— Dr. Seuss

What is the literal sense of Scripture? The *Catechism of the Catholic Church* (no. 116) describes it this way:

> The *literal sense* is the meaning conveyed by the words of Scripture and discovered by exegesis, following the rules of sound interpretation: "All other senses of Sacred Scripture are based on the literal."[1]

In other words, the literal sense of Scripture is that meaning which was intended by the human author and which his words convey when he "meant what he said and said what he meant." Thus, when Matthew tells us "Jesus was born in Bethlehem of Judea in the days of Herod the king" his literal meaning, in Greek, and allowing for idiom, peculiarities of Hebraic expression, cultural differences, wind shear, curvature of the earth and expansion of the Universe is, "Jesus was born in Bethlehem of Judea in the days of

---

[1] St. Thomas Aquinas, *Summa Theologiae*, I,1,10, *ad* 1.

Herod the king." Similarly, when Luke records Jesus saying, "Love your enemies" he may mean a great number of things, but one thing we can be *most* sure he means is, "Jesus said, 'Love your enemies.'"

As the passage from the *Catechism* above indicates, it is absolutely vital, before all else, to know the literal sense of a given passage of Scripture for the same reason that it is absolutely vital that a well-constructed building have a solid foundation. All the other senses of Scripture depend upon understanding the literal sense first. Given that, Pope Pius XII says, "It is the duty of the exegete to lay hold, so to speak, with the greatest care and reverence of the very least expressions which, under the inspiration of the Divine Spirit, have flowed from the pen of the sacred writer, so as to arrive at a deeper and fuller knowledge of his meaning."[2] Likewise, the *Catechism* (no. 109) tells us, "In Sacred Scripture, God speaks to man in a human way. To interpret Scripture correctly, the reader must be attentive to what the human authors truly wanted to affirm and to what God wanted to reveal to us by their words."

All this is smooth sailing and seems fairly obvious. Nonetheless, we must keep in mind that the literal sense of Scripture is often much trickier to discern than we might realize. The reasons for this are numerous. Sometimes, for instance, the problem may lie with a text that is obscure even in the original language. Other times, the problem may lie in the difficulty of translating an idea from Hebrew, Aramaic, or Greek into another language. Still other times, the problem lies with us as readers being unable to cope with some difficulty, slang term, alien mode of ex-

---

[2] Pius XII, *Divino Afflante Spiritu*, 15.

pression, cultural difference, or theological concept which is foreign to our own time and culture. (Recall, for instance, the story we discussed in Chapter 3 of Abraham "cutting a covenant" with God. Without some background as to the meaning of that strange ritual, many modern readers would simply be at sea when they read that text.) Misunderstandings of the literal sense of Scripture therefore can and do abound. The task of the serious student of Scripture is to reduce those misunderstandings as much as possible and to come to a serious and humble encounter with what Scripture is actually saying.

To do this, it is well for the student of Scripture to be forearmed against the common fallacies that can hinder the study of the Bible. Perhaps the most mysterious and widespread of those fallacies is the great, fat, well-swilled nonsensical superstition that Scripture ought always to be "simple." To be sure, there are passages in Scripture that are clear and lucid and speak directly to the heart and soul. One does not need to be a rocket scientist to derive benefit from Psalm 23 or to appreciate the parable of the sheep and goats in Matthew 25. Jesus himself spent little time in the company of scribes and scholars (except to give them a well-deserved kick in the pants when they deluded themselves that they were Something Special because of their knowledge [Matthew 23]). But the mere fact that Jesus rebuked intellectuals for being prideful about their learning is not an especially good argument for becoming prideful about our ignorance.

Sad to say though, some of us Christians are. We fall prey to the idea that there is something meritorious about not wanting to do the hard work of finding out what a biblical author was actually talking about. Some go so far as to treat Scripture as a sort of holy Ouija board, asking it questions about their finances or romances and then sticking their finger onto a page at random and "interpreting" whatever verse pops up as "the word of God to me." Others, only slightly more sophisticated, take passages wildly out of context or radically misunderstand words and then declare, "This is what the Bible means to me and I have the Holy Spirit too." As an example of this, one television evangelist I saw, reading the King James Version of the story of the widow at the Temple whom Jesus commended for "giving out of her *want*" (Luke 21:1–4) emphatically declared that this verse meant she gave in order to get a husband (because that's what the widow would *want*, doncha know). The TV evangelist was completely unaware of — and utterly uninterested in — the fact that "want" meant to the King James Version translators what the word "lack" or "poverty" means today. In short, Jesus actually commended the woman for her generosity with the little she had to give, not for attempting to buy favors from God by donating sufficient quantities to religious "ministries" such as the TV evangelist's. The TV evangelist's exegesis of the passage was not only wrong, it was destructive.

All this sort of thing, which is nearly always palmed off as "letting the Spirit speak to me directly without the interference of man" is, at best, simple laziness and is particularly liable (as the case of our TV evangelist shows) to the temptation to torture Scripture until it says what we want to hear. The idea "Me 'n' My Bible are all I need" is often based on the complete fiction that we are in the exact same circumstances as the simple fisherfolk and villagers Jesus addressed. But the reality is that virtually no one in the modern English-speaking world is in that situation. We are immersed in a vastly different culture from biblical times, replete with a huge stream of information rushing at us 24 hours a day, seven days a week, filled with questions, assumptions, and prejudices which quite simply never entered the heads of the people to whom Jesus spoke. When the Psalmist speaks of the earth being founded on pillars ancient Israelites did not trouble themselves about whether such language was poetry or science. We do. For we — even the least educated of us — know more about geology and cosmology than they did and that knowledge forces us to ask questions of the text that never occurred to the original readers. Similarly, when the original audience read of Joshua slaughtering whole populations of Canaanites to the last man, woman, and child, they were not discomfited by this. We, who live both in the light of Jesus' command to love enemies and in the shadow of the Holocaust, are discomfited and so, once again, cannot help asking questions of Scripture which did not occur to the original readers. Not to mention, of course, the fact that the very attempt to "read Scripture for ourselves" is something that would have been extraordinarily difficult for a first century Palestinian peasant since none of them owned Bibles. For them, Scripture was a thing you *heard* at synagogue (and later, at Church), not a thing you read at home. For most people, acquiring a copy of the Bible for home use would have been like purchasing a family space shuttle. That is why Paul writes in Colossians 4:16: "When this letter has been *read among you*, have it read also in the church of the Laodiceans; and see that you read also the letter from Laodicea." In other words, Scripture was *meant* to come to us through the Church. And, of course, it was meant to be understood the way the author intended it, not the way we happen to *feel* like understanding it today.

Bottom line: in approaching Scripture, as in approaching any book, there is, in the words of Fr. Raymond Brown, S.S., "no substitute for educated effort."[3] This means, as Vatican II taught,[4] there are three things we must take special care to do when approaching Scripture:

1. Be especially attentive "to the content and unity of the whole Scripture";

2. Read the Scripture within "the living tradition of the whole Church"; and,

3. Be attentive to the analogy of faith.

Let's look at these guidelines in depth.

1. Be Especially Attentive to the Content and Unity of the Whole Scripture

The very first step we take as readers in understanding a biblical (or, for that matter, any) text is to determine what literary form the author is employing. Is the passage poetry? Historical narrative? Philosophical reflection? Pastoral instruction? Apocalyptic? Myth? Scripture is simply crammed with a wide variety of different kinds of writing, and the *kind* of writing you are reading will greatly influence the *way* in which it is intended to be read.

---

[3] *The Jerome Biblical Commentary*, Vol. 2, Raymond E. Brown, S.S., Joseph A. Fitzmyer, S.J., Roland E. Murphy, O.Carm., eds., (Englewood Cliffs: Prentice-Hall, 1968), p. 607.

[4] *Dei Verbum*, 12 §4.

It will not, however, affect one tiny bit the question of whether the text has a literal meaning because — mark this — *every biblical text has a literal meaning*. Many people are stunned to hear this. That is because many people think a "literal meaning" can only be conveyed by literal language. They make the mistake of assuming that an author who uses metaphor, fiction, hyperbole, or various other figures of speech does not have a literal meaning. Thus, for instance, if I say "my heart is broken", some people mistakenly imagine that I "meant nothing literally." But, of course, I do. I *literally* mean I am deeply grieved and I am expressing that grief via a metaphor. Likewise, if I say "I stood in line for a million years" I am using an exaggeration to communicate another *literal* meaning: I waited a long time. Indeed, more often than not, metaphor is exactly the right vehicle for conveying a literal meaning and is far better than nonfigurative language. The shortest distance between two minds is a figure of speech.

George Orwell showed this quite clearly when he quoted a well-known verse from Ecclesiastes 9:11:

> I returned and saw under the sun, that the race is not to the swift, nor the battle to the strong, neither yet bread to the wise, nor yet riches to men of understanding, nor yet favour to men of skill; but time and chance happeneth to all of them. [KJV]

. . . and then re-wrote the passage with its life blood drained away and replaced by the embalming fluid of nonfigurative bureaucratic prose:

Objective consideration of contemporary phenomena com-
pels the conclusion that success or failure in competitive
activities exhibits no tendency to be commensurate with
innate capacity, but that a considerable element of the unpredictable must invariably be taken into account.[5]

Both passages have the same literal meaning. But the
original passage breathes while Orwell's "translation" has
all the liveliness of a waxen corpse.

That is why Scripture employs dozens of different devices to communicate literal meanings. "I am the vine and
you are the branches" employs a metaphor to express the
literal meaning of the Christian's complete dependence on
Christ. Likewise, as we saw in Chapter 2, the author of
Genesis uses various linguistic devices (such as measured
Hebrew poetry and the image of six "days" of creation) to
convey a literal meaning, but many modern readers mistake the device for the meaning. The literal sense of the
author was "creation is the orderly act of a loving Creator
God." What the modern reader often hears, however, is
"The universe was made in six twenty-four-hour days."
This is as wrong-headed as taking me to mean I actually
stood in line a million years or that my cardiac tissue has
been torn in half or that Christ had delusions of being a
grape plant. It is necessary therefore to distinguish between
the literal meaning of an author and the various literary
devices he may employ to communicate that meaning.

Take, for instance, the parables of Christ. Jesus tells us
the parable of the prodigal son. In relating this story to
us, does Luke intend as his "literal" sense to tell us a true

---

[5] George Orwell, "Politics and the English Language", *The New Re-
public*, June 17–24, 1946.

story about a historical Palestinian domestic dispute? Obviously not. His literal meaning is "God forgives the repentant sinner." But he has used a particular literary device employed by Christ to get that literal meaning across. Likewise, elsewhere in Scripture, we find writers making continual recourse to metaphor, poetic imagery, fiction and hyperbole to get across a literal meaning.

That is what is happening in the Psalms. Every one of the Psalms is filled with literal meanings. Thus, the literal meaning of Psalm 23 is, "God takes care of us." But the *way* in which the psalm (and all psalms) communicates that literal meaning is by means of a series of metaphors and imagery portraying God as a shepherd and we as a flock of sheep. In the same way, the prophets may speak of God's strong right arm or of the eyes of God watching Israel. They do not, of course, intend to say that God is a man with an anatomy. Rather, their literal meaning is that God is omnipotent and omniscient. But they employ metaphorical language to get their literal meaning across.

Again, this is fairly smooth sailing. But when we get to *fiction* rather than metaphor or parable as the means for conveying a literal sense the waters can sometimes get a little choppier. Good examples of this are books like Tobit or Judith in the Old Testament. For some reason, modern readers who have no difficulty recognizing that the fictional parable of the prodigal son communicates a literal meaning can still stumble over the supposed "difficulty" of Old Testament books that aim to communicate truth via fiction. Thus, when Tobit or Judith are shown to contain a number of historic and geographic inaccuracies, some people get the vapors and imagine this means they could not have been inspired by God.

This is why it is so important to notice what the Church says in the *Catechism* passage above: namely, that we must interpret the books of Scripture "following the rules of sound interpretation." When we do this in the case of Tobit and Judith, we find the Church teaches that to understand the truth of Scripture we have to have in mind *what the author was actually trying to assert*, the *way* he was trying to assert it, and *what is incidental* to that assertion. So, for instance, when the gospels say the women came to the tomb of Jesus at "sunrise", they are not mistakenly asserting the truth of Ptolemaic astronomy or promulgating a dogma that the sun rises rather than the earth moving. The "error" of the gospels here is an illusion because the gospel writers are not making any particular truth claims about astronomy to be in error about. They are simply using human language in a human way.

Similarly, both Judith and Tobit have a number of historical and geographical "errors", not because they are bad history and geography texts, but because they are first rate pious fiction that never pretended to be remotely interested in history or geography any more than the resurrection narratives are interested in astronomy. Indeed, the author of Tobit, in particular, goes out of his way to make *clear* that his hero is fictional. He makes Tobit the uncle of Ahiqar, a figure in ancient Semitic folklore like Jack the Giant Killer or Aladdin. Thus, just as one does not wave a medieval history textbook and complain of a tale that begins "once upon a time when King Arthur ruled the land", so Catholics are not reading Tobit and Judith to get a history lesson. That's not the sort of stories they are and that's not the sort of truth they tell.

The necessity for proper exegesis and the use of sound

rules of interpretation becomes even clearer when we confront the fact that we are reading an ancient text from another culture written in a language foreign to the vast ma-
jority of us. The principal danger of Bible study is not that
we will be mystified by the text, but that we will *think* we
understand the text in the very act of radically misreading
it. A woman I know once took great offense at the story of
Tobit because her casual reading of it convinced her it was
demonic. Why? Because the angel Raphael appears in the
story under a false identity. Angels who lie are demons,
she reasoned. So there you are.

This is, however, to badly misunderstand the kind of
story Tobit is. The author does not mean (nor does his
original audience understand him to mean) "Angels lie. So
should you." On the contrary, Tobit is a classic example
of an "entertaining angels unaware" story (see Hebrews
13:2). We readers *know* who Raphael is all along. When
Tobit cries out to God for help, God immediately answers
him by sending Raphael. But, as is often the case, God's
deliverance is not noticed at first. Raphael introduces himself as "Azariah" (which means "Yahweh helps") and then
names off to Tobit a string of supposed mutual relations,
all with names meaning things like "Yahweh is merciful,"
"Yahweh gives," "Yahweh hears." By this device, the author is saying (with a nudge and a wink) "Psst! Audience!
Get it?" And we, of course, do get it (particularly if we are
listening to the story in the original Hebrew.) Indeed, by
using the name "Yahweh helps", Raphael is not so much
using an alias as revealing the deepest truth about who
God is and why he is here. It is *that* truth and not any
detail about history or geography or the fun of lying that
the author of Tobit aims to tell.

That said, it is necessary to add that while ancient writers of fiction may not be interested in such matters, it is nonetheless necessary for modern students of Scripture to pay attention (as much as the data permits) to the historical, geographical, ethnic, and linguistic circumstances behind the composition of a particular book. So, for instance, it is worth knowing that the gospel of Matthew was composed primarily for a Jewish audience. This would explain why Matthew makes far more frequent allusion to the Old Testament than the other gospels: he is at particular pains to show his audience that Jesus fulfills their Scripture. Matthew is aware of the connections between the Old and New Covenants and, like much of the New Testament, is trying to make these connections clear to his audience.

This explains why the Church urges us to pay attention to the "inner unity" of Scripture. That is, there is an interplay of ideas, concepts, historical references, and terminology between the various authors of Scripture that, under the guidance of the Holy Spirit, creates a certain unity of outlook among authors separated by 1,600 years, several different languages and various other circumstances. We should pay close attention when one inspired author cites another. We should also pay attention when an inspired author cites an *un*inspired author. Note, for example, that Luke is primarily writing for a cultured Greek-speaking Gentile audience that was also familiar with Judaism before becoming Christian, so he not only alludes to the Old Testament, he records Paul quoting Greek poetry.

Likewise, in the Hebrew Scriptures, a knowledge of historical circumstances behind the composition of a given book is critical. If we do not know that the prophecies of Jeremiah concern the fate of the Jews in the years leading up to the Babylonian Captivity, we simply cannot understand what Jeremiah is about. It would be like reading a book about Abraham Lincoln's presidency without knowing anything about the Civil War. In the same way, if we do not know the universal reputation of the Assyrians for their unbelievable brutality and cruelty, much of the impact of the book of Jonah (where God sends a prophet to *save* these monstrous creatures) is lost on us.

Another problem we can have with Scripture is our failure to understand when a text is using a figure of speech to make a point. Thus, if I tell a native speaker of Chinese "Don't count your chickens before they're hatched" I am not giving advice on poultry raising, but I do have a literal meaning: "Don't prematurely assume you know how things will turn out." My Chinese friend, laboring to discern my literal meaning, might labor a long time if he didn't happen to know about English slang and colloquialism. A classic example of this same problem is Jesus' hyperbolic statement, "If your right eye causes you to sin, pluck it out and throw it away; it is better that you lose one of your members than that your whole body be thrown into hell. And if your right hand causes you to sin, cut it off and throw it away; it is better that you lose one of your members than that your whole body go into hell" (Matthew 5:29–30). Jesus is using a dramatic image to convey the need for a pure heart in following God. The literal meaning of the text is "be pure" not "mutilate yourself." Yet there have been, from time to time, Christians who have mistaken the metaphor for the literal sense it was intended to convey. And so, we periodically hear reports of overzealous Christians administering various forms of unpleasant self-surgery in what they imagine to be "obedience" to the supposed "literal" sense of this text.

This leads to another important distinction which needs

to be made when discussing the literal sense of Scripture. In the verse quoted in the paragraph above, Jesus uses the image of hacking off our hands and gouging out our eyes to graphically describe what it is like to renounce cherished sins. It is therefore tempting for many modern readers to conclude from this that, since the rest of the verse is using metaphor to express the literal sense, therefore Jesus must not be speaking literally when he mentions Hell either.

It is precisely here that we must pause and consider the second point made by the Second Vatican Council.

2. Read the Scripture within "the living tradition of the whole Church."

That is, we must ask how a given text has been understood over the span of the Church's history. In the case we happen to be discussing above, that would mean asking whether or not the Church has historically taken the doctrine of Hell literally as well as asking how the rest of Scripture treats the idea of Hell. When we do ask, we find that both Scripture and the subsequent Christian tradition does indeed take the possibility of damnation literally. And we find that the Church does so because our Lord does as well. True, he uses metaphorical language to *describe* Hell (such as "the worm that does not die, and the fire that is not quenched" [Mark 9:48]), but the metaphor points to a literal meaning: that is, to eternal damnation. In short, Jesus really does mean to say that it is possible to cut ourselves off from God for all eternity by freely chosen sin. What is metaphorical is not the doctrine of Hell itself but only the images used to describe it. And the images point to something more, not less, horrible than what they depict.

Conversely, when Jesus speaks of Heaven or eternal life or of our "reward", he really does mean Heaven. And this is verifiable by looking at the unity of Scripture and at the way in which the Church has always traditionally understood Scripture on this point. Heaven is not a metaphor for feeling good about ourselves or accruing the respect of our peers. It means, very literally, everlasting, ecstatic union with God for all eternity. The *imagery* Scripture uses to describe Heaven (white robes, gold, the new Jerusalem, etc.) is, of course, merely imagery. But, again, the images point to something more, not less, wonderful than what they depict.

All this reminds us again that we are to read Scripture as the written aspect of the total Tradition handed on to us "either by word of mouth or by letter" (2 Thessalonians 2:15). For, as we have seen in Chapter 5, the apostles handed down to the Church, not just a book, but an entirely new *Way* (Acts 24:14) of life, teaching, and worship. It was in that environment that the Old Testament was interpreted and the New Testament was written and read. Therefore, if we wish to "get" what Scripture is talking about, it is necessary that we too understand and live in that environment of the Body of Christ in unison with the successors of the apostles and Peter and learn to see the light of Scripture through the lens of the overall apostolic Tradition. When we do, this leads to the third instruction the Vatican Council has provided for us.

3. Be attentive to the analogy of faith.

What *is* the "analogy of faith"? To answer that let us first ask, what's an analogy? An analogy is a thing that resembles, is similar to, or comparable to something else. So, for instance, Jesus made use of many analogies in describing the Kingdom of Heaven. He would say, "The Kingdom of Heaven is like . . ." and then give an analogy. We do the same thing. Elvis sings, "You ain't nothing but a hound dog" and we realize he is employing an analogy, comparing the unfortunate recipient of the song to a hound dog in the way she acts.

Going a little bit further, we note that we sometimes speak of an analog as though it were identical with the thing it resembles. So, for instance, I may point to a photograph (that is, an analog) of my wife and say, "I love her." Even though I point *to* the photograph, I am really, so to speak, pointing *through* it to my wife. The photograph is the *symbol* of what I love, but my wife is the *object* of my love.

Now let us return to the idea of the analogy of faith. From time to time, the Church has found it necessary to confront various questions and difficulties in understanding the apostolic deposit of faith which has come down to it. One classic example of this is the problem which confronted the Church in the early fourth century concerning the person of Christ. Just who is he? For three hundred years the Church had preserved (from the apostles themselves) the general, not-too-carefully-defined faith in Christ as somehow God, yet not the same as God the Father or the Holy Spirit ("The Word was with God and the Word was God" [John 1:1]). At the same time the Church had also been taught by the apostles that there is only one God, not three. Various people made various attempts to reconcile these apparently contradictory data. And in the early third century a man named Arius began preaching a doctrine which he imagined made perfect sense of it all but which, in reality, demoted Jesus to a sort of creaturely godlet and gutted the gospel of its content. This generated enormous controversy and compelled the Church to, once and for all, make a careful examination of its written and unwritten Tradition and define just what it believed about the identity of Christ. The result was the Nicene Creed, which defined the Church's faith in one God who is three consubstantial Persons: the Father, Son, and Holy Spirit. Subsequent controversies led the Church to further refine its beliefs in this and a hundred other areas via various conciliar and papal teachings. These teachings summarize, in a certain sense, "what we believe as Catholics." They are absolutely indispensable in making sense out of the written and unwritten apostolic Tradition handed down to us. Yet, just as the photograph is only a symbol and not the object of my love, so the various creeds and doctrines of the Church — indeed, the Bible itself — are only the symbols or analogies, not the ultimate object, of faith. The Triune God is the ultimate object of faith.

The primary function of the analogy of faith is, therefore, to provide boundaries within which the proper understanding of Scripture and revelation can thrive, not to micromanage our interpretation of each and every verse of the Bible. The Church is, in fact, *disinclined* to define its Tradition unless it absolutely has to. That is why it has so little dogma to show for 2,000 years of activity. But where the Church has definitely spoken, the analogy of faith is essential for helping us get an understanding of the true sense of the text and not run off into the weeds beyond the boundaries of common sense. For the standing temptation of the serious Bible student is often to over-emphasize one biblical text at the expense of other equally important texts. The various doctrines of the Church (always carefully formulated in light of a wide knowledge of written and unwritten Tradition) hold before our eyes the continual necessity to take the whole of Scripture and Tradition seriously when it teaches both that God is one *and* that God is three, that he is sovereign *and* that we have free will, that Jesus is man *and* that Jesus is God as well as a thousand other paradoxes which we, like Arius, are tempted to "resolve" by simply ignoring an inconvenient bit of Scripture in favor of the bit that we "understand." The analogy of faith and the teaching of the Church therefore acts as a critically essential regulator to prevent this temptation to oversimplify from destroying our study of Scripture.

A Note on the Tools of the Trade

To follow the advice of the Second Vatican Council discussed above we will need to avail ourselves of the tools for Bible study. Happily, there are lots of these. They include things like commentaries, concordances, maps, timelines, study Bibles, catechisms, Bible dictionaries, and a host of other helps.[6] Our habit of mind in approaching a given book of Scripture should be to approach it with both reverence and with common sense. That is, we must bear in mind that we are reading a text inspired by the Holy Spirit which is quite literally the word of God. Yet we should also approach it as a word full of grace, not magic. We should bear in mind that, as far as the human author is concerned,

---

[6] The appendix to this book lists a good starter kit of such tools.

he was not clairvoyantly writing with us in mind. When Paul wrote his letter to the Romans and Luke his gospel for Theophilus, they were writing to particular audiences with particular needs, questions, and habits of thought. When Deuteronomy was penned, the thought "How can I make this intelligible to suburban Americans?" was not uppermost in the human writer's mind. Therefore, the modern biblical reader must approach any text of Scripture with the same sort of circumspection we would feel if reading somebody else's love letters, diary, or journal. It is only when we understand what the author was trying to say to his original audience that we can then begin to apply his word to our own lives.

On the other hand, our circumspection must not allow us to imagine that only someone with a Ph.D. can read the Bible. Admittedly, there are biblical critics who fancy that they and they alone know what Scripture says. Some have gone so far as to imagine they can "deconstruct" Scripture to the point that it doesn't say anything at all. And some students of Scripture spend more time reading commentaries and footnotes than the biblical text itself. But this, like the refusal to use any study materials whatsoever, is an extreme.

The healthy middle ground is occupied by the sensible Catholic who bones up on the background, subject and authorship of a given book and who pays attention to the footnotes and cross-references in his Bible which give helpful clues about the historic, cultural, theological, and linguistic information necessary to comprehend its meaning. If he hits a passage that angers, puzzles, or baffles him, his first instinct is not to fling the book across the room or offer some glib "resolution" to the problem, but is rather to see what, if anything, the rest of the Tradition and reliable biblical scholarship has to say about it. And nowhere is this more important than when a passage of Scripture seems to us to "obviously" mean something that is radically at odds with historic Christianity. It is just here that a reliable Catholic study help can do wonders by showing the way in which others have wrestled with the same text with the help of the Holy Spirit. This habit of turning to the Church and its Tradition in order to understand Scripture is completely biblical. Witness, for instance, this incident from the book of Acts:

> And behold, an Ethiopian, a eunuch, a minister of the Candace, queen of the Ethiopians, in charge of all her treasure, had come to Jerusalem to worship and was returning; seated in his chariot, he was reading the prophet Isaiah. And the Spirit said to Philip, "Go up and join this chariot." So Philip ran to him, and heard him reading Isaiah the prophet, and asked, "Do you understand what you are reading?" And he said, "How can I, unless some one guides me?" And he invited Philip to come up and sit with him. Now the passage of the scripture which he was reading was this: "As a sheep led to the slaughter or a lamb before its shearer is dumb, so he opens not his mouth. In his humiliation justice was denied him. Who can describe his generation? For his life is taken up from the earth." And the eunuch said to Philip, "About whom, pray, does the prophet say this, about himself or about some one else?" Then Philip opened his mouth, and beginning with this scripture he told him the good news of Jesus. (Acts 8:27–35)

The Ethiopian eunuch was neither afraid nor ashamed to acknowledge his bafflement at a passage of Scripture.

He asked for help and he got it. Let us, therefore, do the same by making use of the tools God gives us through his holy Church.

Arriving at as clear an understanding as possible of what the original author was trying to say is at the very heart and soul of the literal sense of Scripture. Yet, critical as it is, the literal sense of Scripture is by no means the *only* sense of Scripture. It exists, not to the exclusion of all other senses, but rather, as the *Catechism of the Catholic Church* makes clear, as the *basis* for all other senses. Bearing in mind then the survey of Scripture that we saw in Chapters 1 through 5, let us look at those other senses and see some of the ways in which our Lord and his apostles taught the Church to read its Bible for all it is worth.

7

The Allegorical
Sense of Scripture

This means something. This is important.

— Roy Neary

(Contemplating his sculpted pile of mashed potatoes in Close Encounters of the Third Kind.)

As we mentioned in the last chapter, one of the standing temptations of the biblical student is to oversimplify by seizing on one truth and using it to discount other, equally important truths. One such oversimplification consists of the habit some modern people have of exalting the primacy of the literal sense of Scripture into a flat denial of the possibility of any other senses of Scripture at all. This posture of "liberal fundamentalism" says, in effect, "The human author said it. There's nothing more to it. That settles it." According to this notion, all attempts to seek any second meanings in Scripture are to be dismissed (in the words of one modern scholar[1]) as "a sort of weasel word" whereby

---

[1] J. A. Fitzmyer, S.J., quoted in Scott Hahn: "Coming to Our Senses: Rediscovering the Lost Art of Spiritual Exegesis", *Lay Witness*, September 1998, p. 6.

the reader can make the biblical text mean anything he likes.

This denial of a second sense in Scripture can lead to curious results, as a friend of mine discovered one evening watching one of those "Mysteries of the Bible" shows on TV. On the show were a couple of theologians eager to get their fifteen minutes of fame. So rather than talk about the Faith, they obligingly told the camera that Jesus was not born of a virgin and based their claim on the allegation that St. Matthew misunderstood the prophet Isaiah.

It's like this, said the scholars: A couple of centuries after Isaiah wrote, the Hebrew Bible (including the book of Isaiah) was translated into Greek (since many Jews were spread over the Greek-speaking ancient world and were forgetting their Hebrew just as European immigrants to the United States forgot their Yiddish in an English-speaking culture). This Greek translation of the Hebrew Bible (that is, the Old Testament) is called the Septuagint.

Now in the original Hebrew text of Isaiah 7:14 we read the prophecy that "the 'almah' shall conceive and bear a son, and you shall call his name 'Immanuel.'" "Almah" means in Hebrew "young woman" and refers to any young woman, virgin or not. But when the Jewish translators of the Septuagint translated Isaiah into Greek (decades before the birth of Christ), they did not translate the term as "young woman" but as "parthenos" which means "virgin." Later on, after Christ comes, St. Matthew is reading this Greek translation, not the original Hebrew when he declares of the Virgin Birth, "All this took place to fulfil what the Lord had spoken by the prophet: 'Behold, a virgin shall conceive and bear a son, and his name shall be called Emmanuel.'" But, said the TV theologians, we now know

St. Matthew was mistaken to believe in the Virgin Birth since Isaiah did not say "virgin" but "young woman."

So my friend was wrestling with what seemed an inevitable set of conclusions: a) the Septuagint translation is flat wrong; b) Matthew was ignorant of the actual meaning of Isaiah; c) he therefore *derived* his belief in the Virgin Birth from a mistaken translation of Isaiah and d) the Church therefore erred in defining its dogma of the Virgin Birth of Christ by mistakenly seeing a second "spiritual" meaning in the text of Isaiah when, in reality, there was (and could only be) Isaiah's original, literal meaning.

This is however, to enter into a whole complex of mistakes, not clarifications. To find out what's *really* going on, let's look again at the New Testament use of Old Testament Scripture.

The first and most obvious point in the New Testament, as we saw in Chapter 5, is that Jesus Christ is the fulfillment of the Old Testament. The apostles came to believe this, not because they saw the Virgin Birth, but because they saw the risen Christ. And the risen Christ, as we saw previously, is the one who did not come to abolish the law and the prophets but to fulfill them (Matthew 5:17) and, after his resurrection, tells his disciples that "Moses and all the prophets" had written "concerning himself" (Luke 24:26–27). This is where the apostles get the idea that the whole life and ministry of Christ "fulfilled the Scriptures." So far so good.

What is not so good however is that it is easy for the modern reader to adopt a kind of "checklist" mentality about messianic prophecy, as though every first-century Jew had an agreed-upon set of "Messianic Verses" in the Old Testament against which all messianic claimants were measured. Indeed, many books of Christian apologetics today[2] lay out precisely this sort of schema:

Prophecy:	*Source*	*Fulfillment*
The Messiah must be . . .	(OT)	(NT)
born in Bethlehem	Mic. 5:1	Matt. 2:1; Lk. 2:4–7
adored by great persons	Ps. 72:10–11	Matt. 2:1–11
sold for 30 pieces of silver	Zech. 11:12	Matt. 26:15

and so forth. One could easily get the impression that all a first-century Jew had to do was follow Jesus around, ticking off prophecy fulfillments on his Old Testament Messianic Prophecy Checklist and he ought to have known everything that Jesus was going to do before he ever did it.

But, as we have seen, the New Testament makes plain that the prophecies of Messiah were not so much *revealed* by the Old Testament as they were *hidden* there. This is precisely why St. Paul writes that the New Covenant was "veiled" until the gospel took away the veil (2 Corinthians 3:14). It is also why he declares the gospel was "*not* made known to men in other generations as it has now been revealed by the Spirit to God's holy apostles and prophets" (Ephesians 3:5). In short, Paul insists the deepest meaning of the Old Testament was seen only *after* the life, death and resurrection of Christ.

This is why nobody before these events says, "Why, it's

---

[2] I take the example below from *The Jewish New Testament*, tr. David H. Stern (Clarksville: Jewish New Testament Publications, 1989), pp. xxvi–xxix. One can also find the same sort of checklist in some of the works by Josh McDowell.

plain from Scripture that the Messiah will be born of a virgin, rejected by the chief priests, handed over to Gentiles, crucified with thieves, risen, ascended, and that he will abrogate the circumcision demand for Gentiles as he breaks down the barrier between man and woman, slave and free, Jew and Gentile." Even the disciples themselves, close as they were to Jesus, make it clear they did not anticipate the crucifixion, much less the resurrection, one little bit — even when Jesus rubbed their noses in it (Mark 9:9–10). As John says, they did *not* understand from the Scripture that the Messiah had to rise from the dead, even while they were standing in the mouth of the empty tomb gawking at his graveclothes (John 20:1–10).

And yet, these same apostles speak of the resurrection (like the Virgin Birth) as a "fulfillment" of the prophecies. What then do they mean if they do not mean the prophecies were "predictions" which everybody based their understanding of Messiah upon?

They mean that Christ fulfilled, brought to fruition, and was the ultimate Case in Point toward which all the Old Testament was straining and pointing. They mean he was the One toward whom the law and prophets were being pointed by his Spirit even when the sacred writers themselves did not know quite what they were pointing toward (1 Peter 1:10–11). This is why the early Church never had difficulty with an issue which often vexes modern minds: namely, why the New Testament often takes Old Testament texts out of their immediate context and sees them as applicable to Christ. For the early Church does not see the Old Testament as talking about something different from Christ, but rather sees it in relationship to him. What appear to us to be separate themes and events in the Old Testament, appear to the New Testament writers as so many spokes on a wheel all connected to the Hub who is Christ.

So, for instance, Hebrews 2:13 quotes Isaiah 8:18: "Here I am, and the children God has given me." In its *literal sense*, Isaiah is speaking about his own disciples with no hint of messianic intent behind these words. Yet the author of Hebrews sees *Christ*, far more than Isaiah, fulfilling the text. Why? Because Christ and his Church are, most fully, what Isaiah and his disciples were in a kind of foreshadow. The words of the book of Isaiah, like all words, are signs signifying something, in this case Isaiah and his own disciples. But Isaiah and his own disciples are, in their turn, *also* signs signifying something even greater: Christ and his Church. For Christ and his Church are the ultimate Case in Point of what Isaiah and his disciples were: "signs and portents in Israel from the Lord of hosts, who dwells on Mount Zion" (Isaiah 8:18). Isaiah and his disciples do indeed fulfill the passage in an immediate and literal sense. But the early Church sees no particular reason why this forbids the God whom Isaiah worshipped from fulfilling it even more profoundly when He becomes incarnate and establishes his Church. Therefore the author of Hebrews, reading the Isaian passage with hindsight through the lens of the entire life and ministry of Christ, sees an allegory hidden in it by God of which Isaiah himself knew nothing.

Likewise, with Isaiah 7:14, we find that the passage has a much more immediate fulfillment than the birth of Christ. The Immanuel Prophecy comes in an hour of national crisis during the reign of Ahaz, one of the lousier kings of Judah and descendants of David. The northern kingdom of Israel has formed an alliance with Syria against Ahaz' southern kingdom of Judah and as a result the Judeans are in a muck sweat about the future of their country. So Isaiah goes to Ahaz, tells him not to worry about the alliance since God will take care of Judah, and offers Ahaz the chance to "ask a sign of the Lord your God" (Isaiah 7:11) to assure him that everything will be fine. Ahaz refuses, ostensibly because he is too pious to put God to the test, but really because he does not want to obey Isaiah. It is then that the Immanuel Prophecy is given: "Behold the *almah* shall conceive and bear [or 'is with child and shall bear'] a son, and shall call his name Immanuel [which means 'God with us']." What does Isaiah mean?

Most immediately and literally, Isaiah seems to have in mind the promise of a successor to Ahaz, namely Hezekiah, who will carry on the line of David so that, as Nathan had prophesied to David long ago "your throne shall be established forever" (2 Samuel 7:16). In other words, Isaiah is telling Ahaz that "God is with" the Davidic throne still and his kingdom will not be defeated by the menacing alliance to the north. And this prophecy is fulfilled. The menacing alliance against Judah fails and Hezekiah is born. The prophecy in its most immediate sense is fulfilled, not by a *virgin* birth, but by the pregnancy of the wife of Ahaz and the birth of a new "son of David" to carry on the Davidic line.

However, there remains in pre-Christian Jewish tradition a persistent belief in larger and second meanings in its Bible. As we have seen, there is, for instance, a growing sense that the prophecy of Nathan to David in 2 Samuel 7 (despite these immediate fulfillments) speaks not so much of an everlasting political rule, but of some higher and greater Throne. That is why, when the political rule of the house of David finally *does* fail, Israel continues to remember Nathan's words and wonders what deeper meaning they might have. In the same way, Israel is told to await a Prophet by Moses (Deuteronomy 18:15) and, indeed, many prophets appear. Yet Israel, instead of seeing them as the final fulfillment of Moses' promise, instead comes to believe that some Great and Ultimate Prophet is coming; an august Somebody of whom the Old Testament Prophets are just dim images or foreshadows. This is why the Jews asked John the Baptist if he was "*The* Prophet" (John 1:21). And so, as we have seen, the Jews slowly develop over time the strong belief that there is, in the Bible, a mysterious inner meaning as well as the slowly dawning awareness that Somebody is coming — some Anointed One or Servant or Prophet or Son of David or Son of Man (the titles are fuzzy in the Old Testament) — who will make clear the tantalizing hints and "utter things hidden since the creation of the world" (Matthew 13:35).

There is then, both clarity *and* obscurity concerning the messianic message of the Old Testament in the time of Christ. Certain texts (like the prophecy of Nathan concerning the covenant with David) are clearly understood by most Jews to be messianic. Yet at the same time, other passages are never dreamed of as referring to a Messiah until *after* Jesus of Nazareth's astounding career is over. Nobody understands Psalms 69 and 109 beforehand as a prophecy of the Election of Matthias to the office vacated by Judas, nor understands the unbroken bones of the Passover lamb as a prophetic image of Christ's unbroken bones, nor sees in advance that Isaiah 53 bears witness to the crucifixion and resurrection. If they had, says St. Paul, they would never have crucified the Lord of Glory (1 Corinthians 2:8). All these things are only seen *after the fact* as eerily prophetic of Christ and his Church. They fill out the picture dimly sketched by the more widely acknowledged messianic prophecies, but only in hindsight.

This is why, rather than viewing their Hebrew Bibles as a source of proof texts to be strung together into a checklist, the early Christians see the Old Testament *bearing inspired witness* to the extraordinary man who had dwelt among them. They did not, for instance, read "Zeal for thy house will consume me" in Psalm 69 and then decide "Let's believe Jesus cleansed the Temple because of this verse." On the contrary, Jesus cleanses the Temple *first* (John 2:13–16) and then afterwards his disciples *remember* the verse and are struck by how it "fits" the event. This happens again and again in the New Testament. The disciples are as surprised as anybody else when Jesus heals the sick or raises the dead. They do not foresee the miracles of Christ by reading the Old Testament. Rather, the ministry of Christ happens and they then see an uncanny connection between what Jesus does and the weird way in which it fits the Old Testament. When Jesus is sold for 30 pieces of silver or his hands and feet are pierced on the Cross, the apostles do not discover this by sticking their noses into the book of Zechariah or Psalm 22. Rather, after Jesus is raised, they *remember* that these things were written and, blinking their eyes in amazement, say "It was staring us in the face all along and we didn't see it!" The Old Testament is not the *basis* of their belief in these things, it is the *witness* to these things.

And so, back to my friend and his worries about the Virgin Birth. First off, the translators of the Septuagint did not make a "wrong" translation of "almah" into "parthenos." Recall that the translation was made just a little bit before the sexual revolution in the 1960s. Hence, it was commonly assumed in the culture of the translators that a young woman, assuming she was unmarried, would also be a virgin. The translators of the Septuagint, faced with a choice between the Greek word for "young woman" and Greek word for "virgin" opted, for whatever mysterious reasons, to use the latter. From a purely linguistic viewpoint, it was not the smartest move in the world. But neither was it wildly beyond the pale. Words seldom mean one thing and one thing only.

Second, whatever may have been the mistaken (or was it providential?) motivations of the Septuagint translators, Matthew did not, in any event, *derive* his belief in Mary's virginity from Isaiah 7:14. He did not sit down one day, read Isaiah, and say to himself, "Let's see. Isaiah says something about a virgin here. So if I'm going to cook up a Christ figure, I'd better make him the son of a virgin so it'll fit with this text." On the contrary, the apostles encounter a man who does extraordinary things like rising from the dead and, when they inquire about his origins — which they could only have known if Mary or Jesus volunteered them — find he was born of a virgin. They *then* look at their Septuagint Bibles, run across this weird passage in the Greek text of Isaiah and see him *reflected* in this verse (because Jesus had told them that the law and the prophets are, in their deepest sense, about him). The Church's faith in the virginity of Mary originates *not* in a textual misunderstanding, but in the historical fact of the Virgin Birth of Christ to which the Septuagint translation bears curiously providential witness. The basis of the Church's Faith, then as now, is Jesus Christ himself.

The Allegorical Sense of Scripture in Practice

Now, as we saw in Chapters 1 through 5, Jesus, his apostles, and his Church after him have made copious use of the allegorical sense of Scripture. We noted, for instance, that Jesus tells us in John 6 that the manna in the wilderness is an image of himself, the bread of life. Likewise, Paul tells the Corinthians that the passage through the Red Sea is an image of baptism. Similarly, Hebrews spends a considerable amount of ink drawing allegorical lessons from the Old Testament descriptions of the tabernacle. And, of course, our little study simply scratched the surface of the allegorical significance which the New Testament finds in the Old. The New Testament is absolutely steeped in Jewish Scripture and sees a huge array of people, images, and events as signs pointing to Christ and his Church.

The modern reader, however, quite rightly approaches Scripture with a certain amount of trepidation. We are not, after all, inspired biblical writers. What may seem to us "deeply spiritual" in a given text may in fact be mere moonshine or wishful thinking. Likewise, what seems to us prosaic might in fact be laden with a significance to which we are blind. How then are we to discern "second meanings" in Scripture without walking off into the weeds and getting silly?

The first and most important thing to remember is that, as Catholics, we do not need to reinvent the wheel. As with the literal sense of Scripture, the apostles have already handed down to us a Tradition and Church which has done a huge amount of the work long before we were born. This does not mean there is nothing for us to do. But it does mean that the outline of sanity in biblical interpretation has already been clearly sketched for us.

Of course, the boldest and clearest lines in allegorical interpretation are sketched in the New Testament itself. Jesus and the apostles hold our hands and walk us through a wide variety of allegorical readings of Scripture. And so, for instance, we are explicitly told that the ladder of angels Jacob saw in Genesis 28:12 is an image of Christ (John 1:51). Likewise, Christ explicitly declares (John 3:14) that he is prefigured in the Bronze Serpent in Numbers 21:9. Similarly, Paul tells us in Galatians 4:21–31 that Hagar and Sarah can be fruitfully understood as images of the old and new covenants. And so on through connection after connection in both the gospels and the rest of the New Testament. Since it is the God-Man himself and his inspired apostles and evangelists who are doing the interpreting for us, we can be absolutely sure that these allegorical readings of Scripture are legitimate. If a commentary or "Mysteries of the Bible" pundit tries to sell us the Brooklyn Bridge by declaring such interpretations mistaken or false or by declaring that all allegorical readings of Scripture are invalid, they simply have to take it up with the incarnate Son of God and the ones to whom he said "he who hears you hears me" (Luke 10:16). A God-Man has more impressive credentials than a Ph.D.

Beyond connections explicitly made within the text of Scripture itself, however, are further connections which Scripture does not spell out yet which the subsequent apostolic Tradition of the Church has made extremely clear. In our study, we alluded to some of these and showed the way in which explicit biblical teaching on one point throws stark light on implicit biblical teaching in other areas. So, for instance, although John does not post a big neon sign flashing "I am now making reference to the creation of Eve in Genesis 2" when he describes the piercing of Christ's side we discussed in Chapter 5, nonetheless the connection is hard *not* to see given a) Scripture's constant comparison of Christ with Adam; b) John's focus on Jesus and Mary at the wedding at Cana as the archetypal "sign" of Christ's work; c) John's own habit of speaking of the Church as "the Bride" (Revelation 22:17); and, d) the energetic hand-waving and gesturing John engages in at the point in his narrative where Christ's side is pierced (John 19:34–35). Like any good storyteller, he makes some connections for his audience explicitly but also leaves a huge number of things implicit with the understanding that his audience already knows what he's talking about.

This is, in fact, the habit of most of the biblical writers. They leave a great number of allegorical connections between the Old and New Testaments to be made by their readers. But they also leave the connections clear enough that it is, again, hard not to see them once they're pointed out. Take, for instance, Mary and the Ark of the Covenant. Both Luke and the book of Revelation subtly but very clearly identify Mary with the Ark of the Covenant, wherein dwelt the Presence of God. Luke 1:35, for instance, quotes the angel as saying, "The Holy Spirit will come upon you, and the power of the Most High will overshadow you." This is an allusion to the Shekinah glory which "overshadowed" the Tabernacle and the Ark in the Old Testament (Numbers 9:15). Likewise, "When Elizabeth heard the greeting of Mary, the babe [John the Baptist] leaped in her womb" (Luke 1:41) just as when David brought the Ark to Jerusalem he "danced before the Lord with all his might" (2 Samuel 6:14). And when Mary meets Elizabeth, Elizabeth wonders, "Why is this granted me, that the mother of my Lord should come to me? (Luke 1:43) just as David wondered, "How can the ark of the Lord come to me?" (2 Samuel 6:9). John also makes this connection in his Revelation, where we see first the Ark of the Covenant (Revelation 11:19) and then immediately afterward we see an image of a woman clothed with the sun who gives birth to a "male child, who will rule all the nations with an iron scepter" (Revelation 12:5). The connection between Mary and the Ark, once it is made, is hard not to see. Knowing the identity of Mary's "male child," it would be an easy mental connection for any pious Jew to immediately think of her as a kind of Second Ark. And, not surprisingly, this is precisely what post-apostolic liturgy does.[3]

All this means, once again, that it is necessary for the student of Scripture to pay attention, not only to what Scripture is up to as it makes its various connections, but also to pay attention to the overall Tradition of the Church. One extremely useful way to do this is to note the connections made in the liturgy and prayers of the Church. Every Old Testament and gospel reading in the mass is connected, and the connection is often an allegorical one.

So, for instance, the readings for December 19th (which are right smack in the middle of Advent and are therefore meant to put us in mind of all the events leading up to the birth of Christ) focus on Samson and then upon John

---

[3] Thus the Akathist hymn (an Eastern liturgy in honor of Mary) reads in part, "Hail, O Tabernacle of God the Word. . . . Hail, O Ark that the Spirit has gilded!" Many Eastern hymns use similar language, calling Mary "temple," "tabernacle," "shrine," and so forth. The Akathist hymn can be found in the *Byzantine Book of Prayer* (Pittsburgh: Byzantine Seminary Press; 1995), p. 344.

the Baptist. Why these two figures? Because Samson, like John, is dedicated to God with a Nazirite vow and stands as a kind of dim foreshadow of John. Luke records the vow but does not make the connection between John and Samson explicit. He leaves it for his readers to do that.

Likewise, one of the Old Testament readings for Trinity Sunday draws on Proverbs 8. In that passage, the author's literal sense is to describe the wisdom of God using the literary device of personification. That is, the author of Proverbs portrays Wisdom as a character who takes center stage and delivers a monologue saying, in part:

> "The LORD begot me, the firstborn of his ways,
>   the forerunner of his prodigies of long ago;
> From of old I was poured forth,
>   at the first, before the earth." (Proverbs 8:22–23 [NAB])

Nothing in the New Testament explicitly instructs the Church to "Read Proverbs 8 as a veiled reference to the Blessed Trinity." But several passages in Scripture speak of Christ as "the only begotten Son," the Logos who was "with God in the beginning," and as "the power of God and the *wisdom* of God" (John 3:16; 1:2; 1:24, 30). Once those connections have been made, it is not very hard to see the Holy Spirit speaking through the author of Proverbs in a veiled way about the Trinitarian nature of the God who has now been fully revealed in Jesus Christ. And so, not surprisingly, the Church on Trinity Sunday couples Proverbs 8 with John 16:12–15 which describes how the man who is Wisdom Incarnate will pour out his Spirit of Wisdom from the Father on his disciples:

> "I have yet many things to say to you, but you cannot bear them now. When the Spirit of truth comes, he will

guide you into all the truth; for he will not speak on his own authority, but whatever he hears he will speak, and he will declare to you the things that are to come. He will glorify me, for he will take what is mine and declare it to you. All that the Father has is mine; therefore I said that he will take what is mine and declare it to you.

Once again, a passage with a literal meaning out of the Old Testament is seen — in light of the incarnation, crucifixion, resurrection, ascension, and outpouring of the Spirit of Christ — to have a vastly richer meaning than the human author ever dreamed of. The literal meaning is not damaged or negated any more than the literal meaning of Exodus is negated by seeing the manna in the wilderness as a sign of the Eucharist. It merely takes on fuller dimensions as a square takes on fuller dimensions when it becomes a cube.

In addition to the allegorical readings presented to us in Scripture and in the liturgy and prayers of the Church, there is also the rich store of exegesis handed down to us by the theologians and exegetes throughout the history of the Church. St. Bernard of Clairvaux,[4] for instance, notes the continual use of marriage as one of the primal images of the relationship between Christ and the Church and performs an elaborate allegorical exegesis of the Song of Songs as an image of Christ and his Bride the Church. The original author of the Song does not, of course, literally intend to speak of Christ and his Church. Very possibly, the Song was composed for an actual royal wedding feast. Yet, if this *is* the case, it should nonetheless be noted that, long

---

[4] G. R. Evans, tr., *Bernard of Clairvaux: Selected Works* (New York: Paulist Press, 1987).

before the birth of Christ, the Jewish people themselves interpreted the Song as a portrayal of the relationship between Israel and God under the figure of a marriage, just as prophets like Hosea had done.[5] Thus, it is not altogether surprising that, once again, in light of the full revelation of Christ (and particularly of the sacrament of marriage instituted by Christ) a Catholic reader like St. Bernard will see Christ and his Church hidden in the Song.

In similar ways, other great Christians throughout history have mined the Bible for other insightful allegorical connections. Take honey for instance. The Torah repeatedly describes the Promised Land as a land "flowing with milk and honey" (see Exodus 3:17, Leviticus 20:24, Numbers 13:27, Deuteronomy 27:3, among many other instances). Honey is the yummiest, most scrumptious thing in the entire biblical lexicon. Not surprisingly then, it becomes one of the central biblical images for exquisite luxury, delight, and bounty — a sweetness that can only point to the even greater sweetness of its Creator. It is, therefore, an entirely natural thing for the Psalmist to write: "The ordinances of the Lord are true and righteous altogether. More to be desired are they than gold. . . Sweeter also than honey and drippings of the honeycomb" (Psalm 19:9–10). To Israelite families, this was more than metaphor. When parents taught a child to read, they would have him recite the law of Moses. As he finished, they would give junior a spoonful of honey. This rite of passage sealed in the child,

---

[5] *The Jerome Biblical Commentary*, Vol. 2, Raymond E. Brown, S.S., Joseph A. Fitzmyer, S.J., Roland E. Murphy, O.Carm., eds., (Englewood Cliffs: Prentice-Hall, 1968), p. 507. "The oldest interpretation [of the Song of Songs], in both Christian and Jewish tradition, is religious."

in both body and memory, the exquisite sweetness of God's word.

Thus, not a New Testament writer, but Hippolytus of Rome (in the third century) sees in the scriptural use of honey a figure, "meaning divine doctrine, which restores the spiritual knowledge of the soul."[6] And Clement of Alexandria (also in the third century) builds on this insight, identifying honey not just with doctrine, but with the Divine Teacher himself. Honey, wrote Clement, "seems to have been spoken of the Word, who is honey. Prophecy often extols him above honey and the honeycomb."[7] Then, going back to Scripture in light of this train of thought we notice something: the manna in the desert (which, as we have already seen, is an image of Eucharist) was compared to "wafers made with honey" (Exodus 16:31). And so we find an image in Scripture which reflects reality: The Eucharist both sustains and *delights* us.

Note what is happening here. Our insight into the second meanings of Scripture is not taking place in a vacuum. We are not, like lunatics or tea leaf readers, simply snatching texts at random and making them arbitrarily mean whatever we like. Rather, we are paying attention to the slow, organic growth of an idea which both puts down roots in the whole of Scripture and throws out branches through the history of the Church. That is the way all healthy exegesis proceeds.

Discovering the allegorical sense of Scripture is, like all things Catholic, the fruit of balance, persistence, and most especially, a careful attention to the whole of the written

---

[6] Hippolytus of Rome, *On Proverbs*.
[7] Clement of Alexandria, *Paedagogus*, Book I, Chapter VI.

and unwritten Tradition handed down to us by the apostles in union with the Church. On one hand, the Church teaches the primacy of the literal sense of Scripture and reminds us that all second meanings depend on the literal sense. Thus, we cannot as Catholics simply read into the Bible whatever we like. On the other hand, the Church also reminds us that there really are second meanings to Scripture and we therefore cannot automatically dismiss an allegorical reading as mere fantasy. Rather, we must firmly resolve to place our feet on the road walked by Jesus, his apostles, and so many other saints and scholars of Scripture to find the myriad ways in which God has spoken through his word.

But, of course, to follow Jesus down that road means that we must walk as he did. And to do that, we must explore another of the senses of Scripture: the moral sense.

8

The Moral
Sense of Scripture

*In the New Law, whatever our Head has done is a type
of what we ought to do. Therefore, so far as the things of
the Old Law signify the things of the New Law, there is
the allegorical sense; so far as the things done in Christ, or
so far as the things which signify Christ, are types of what
we ought to do, there is the moral sense.*

— St. Thomas Aquinas

As we saw in the last chapter, Jesus clearly taught that
he did not come to abolish the law and the prophets but to
fulfill them. In looking at the allegorical sense of Scripture,
we have examined some of the ways in which the person
of Christ and the mystery of his Church is foreshadowed
and hidden in the Old Testament. But Scripture does not
merely speak of the *identity* of Jesus and his Church. It
also speaks of what Jesus *does* and of what he demands his
disciples do. For the disciple of Jesus is not merely someone who believes a particular thing *about* Jesus, but someone who must live and act in a particular way *like* Jesus.
That means that Christianity, like Judaism from which it
springs, necessarily entails the teaching of a particular sort
of morality and ethics.

Now, as we mentioned previously, the moral teaching of the New Testament is, in some ways, not wildly different from the Old Testament, nor is it even wildly different from that of Confucius, an Eskimo, or an average Joe. That is because God, as the author of nature, as well as the inspirer of the Old Testament, does not need to scrap his entire project of revelation via natural law and the old covenant and start from scratch with the inauguration of the new covenant. Rather, as is his custom, his grace *perfects* nature rather than abolishing it. And so, where natural law and ordinary human conscience (given us by God) admonish us in general ways to be fair, share our cookies, and not pull our baby sister's hair, the New Testament has no particular comments of rebuttal to offer. Jesus essentially ratifies the rudiments of basic human morality known to us by natural revelation.

In addition, he largely (though with some significant modifications which we will discuss presently) endorses the moral teaching given to Israel. That is why blasphemy, adultery, dishonoring the Sabbath, and general failure to "love the Lord with all your heart, mind, soul, and strength" are as frowned upon (and their opposite virtues are as celebrated) by the new covenant as by the old. Jesus himself makes clear that "till heaven and earth pass away, not an iota, not a dot, will pass from the law until all is accomplished. Whoever then relaxes one of the least of these commandments and teaches men so, shall be called least in the kingdom of heaven; but he who does them and teaches them shall be called great in the kingdom of heaven" (Matthew 5:18–19). Thus, when the rich young man comes to him seeking entry to the kingdom of God Jesus tells him, "You know the commandments: 'Do not commit adultery, Do not kill, Do not steal, Do not bear false witness, Honor your father and mother" (Luke 18:20). Likewise, in the parable of Lazarus and the rich man, the moral of the story is *not* that the rich man should have gone off to some remote country and learned an esoteric philosophy that could have saved his soul. Rather, it is that he should have paid attention to "Moses and the Prophets" when he had the chance (Luke 16:29–31). This is why C. S. Lewis says one of the rewards of reading the Old Testament regularly is that

> You keep on discovering more and more what a tissue of quotations from it the New Testament is; how constantly Our Lord repeated, reinforced, continued, refined, and sublimated, the Judaic ethics, how very seldom He introduced a novelty. This of course was perfectly well-known — was indeed axiomatic — to millions of unlearned Christians as long as Bible reading was habitual. Nowadays it seems to be so forgotten that people think they have somehow discredited Our Lord if they can show that some pre-Christian document (or what they take to be pre-Christian) such as the Dead Sea Scrolls has "anticipated" Him. As if we suppose Him to be a cheapjack like Nietzsche inventing a new ethics! Every good teacher, within Judaism as without, has anticipated Him. The whole religious history of the pre-Christian world, on its better side, anticipates Him. It could not be otherwise. The Light which has lightened every man from the beginning may shine more clearly but cannot change. The Origin cannot suddenly start being, in the popular sense of the word, "original".[1]

---

[1] C. S. Lewis, *Reflections on the Psalms*, (Harcourt, Brace & Jovanovich, Inc.: New York, 1958), pp. 26–27.

All this means that in looking for the "moral sense" of Scripture we should not overlook the obvious: namely, the ordinary, garden variety, didactic moral teaching of the Old and New Testaments. That is, we should — as ever — give primary attention to the literal sense of Scripture and the morality its inspired authors lay out for us in plain language. The fundamentals of this moral teaching are, for the Church as well as for the Synagogue, found in the Ten Commandments, just as the fundamentals of Christian Faith are summed up in the Creed, and the fundamentals of Christian prayer are summed up in the Our Father.

That said, we can also point out that straightforward didactic moral instruction is by no means the only way Scripture communicates its morality and ethics. And so, for centuries Christians have understood Scripture to communicate its moral teachings via many other means as well. Let's explore some of them.

Things Done by *Christ*

On the evening before his death, Jesus "rose from supper, laid aside his garments, and girded himself with a towel. Then he poured water into a basin, and began to wash the disciples' feet, and to wipe them with the towel with which he was girded" (John 13:4–5). In so doing, he offered his disciples not a sermon or concept but a *picture*. It was the picture of their Lord and Master taking the place of a slave. And the point of the picture was simple: "I have given you an example, that you also should do as I have done to you" (John 13:15).

Jesus frequently taught with pictures. As we have seen,

he used verbal pictures in his parables to teach about the nature of the kingdom of God. Here, he used a physical picture — almost an icon — to enact, rather than merely preach about, the way he wished us to live. This was a commonplace, not only of his ministry, but of his life. God the Father ordained not only that his actions, but the very *circumstances* of his life, would be iconographic. The various scenes of the gospels can be described as a series of icons of Christ, little windows or snapshots allowing us to peer *through* Christ into the light from whence he came. And so, for instance, in the gospel of Luke we find that, not just the teaching and miracles of Christ, but even the so-called "accidents" of his life continually point us toward imitating his life of Eucharistic self-giving and to Christ's demand that his disciples, like himself, pour out their lives in continual self-sacrificial love as his body and blood are poured out for the Church.

To get the hang of what I mean consider this: as we have already seen, the miraculous multiplication of loaves and fishes is a sign or icon initiated by Christ which points to the Eucharist. Similarly, the verbal teachings of Christ about his demand for self-sacrificial, eucharistic love are clear. "Whoever loses his life for my sake, he will save it" says Jesus in Luke 9:23. And in case anyone misses the connection between "losing life", "salvation" and Eucharist Jesus spells it out:

> And he took bread, and when he had given thanks he broke it and gave it to them, saying, "This is my body which is given for you. Do this in remembrance of me." And likewise the cup after supper, saying, "This cup which is poured out for you is the new covenant in my blood. (Luke 22:19–21)

Further, Jesus (and his evangelist Luke) very pointedly refer us to the Eucharist in Luke's resurrection account when it is recorded how the risen Christ went unrecognized by his own disciples until that shocking moment when — repeating the identical gesture he made at the Last Supper — Christ "took the bread and blessed, and broke it, and gave it to them. And their eyes were opened and they recognized him" (Luke 24:30–31). These eucharistic connections, once they are pointed out, are again difficult *not* to see. But the intriguing thing is, it is not just these verbal and nonverbal signs which Christ consciously performed that refer us to the Eucharist, but even the "accidents" of his life over which, humanly speaking, he had no control. And so, for instance, Luke is careful to record that Jesus — the Bread of Life — was born in a town called Bethlehem (a name which means "House of Bread") and laid in a manger (that is, a *feed box*). In other words, it is not just the events and words consciously orchestrated by Jesus which provide us with pictures of his gospel, it is *everything* about his life. And so, we his disciples are provided with this wide variety of icons as well as words not only to contemplate, but to somehow imitate.

Obviously, we cannot arrange the circumstances of our own births as God the Son could do, but we can imitate the divine humility of the one who

> though he was in the form of God, did not count equality with God a thing to be grasped, but emptied himself, taking the form of a servant, being born in the likeness of men. And being found in human form he humbled himself and became obedient unto death, even death on a cross. (Philippians 2:6–8)

And so, the apostles trace in this pattern of divine humility the very outline of the life of the Church and instruct their disciples to live accordingly. Paul, for example, passes directly from the hymn in the previous paragraph to giving the Philippian flock a moral instruction based upon it:

> Do all things without grumbling or questioning, that you may be blameless and innocent, children of God without blemish in the midst of a crooked and perverse generation, among whom you shine as lights in the world, holding fast the word of life, so that in the day of Christ I may be proud that I did not run in vain or labor in vain. Even if I am to be poured as a libation upon the sacrificial offering of your faith, I am glad and rejoice with you all. Likewise you also should be glad and rejoice with me. (Philippians 2:14–18)

Paul tells us we are to "shine as lights in the world." In so doing, he puts us in mind of two sayings of Jesus: "*I* am the light of the world" and "*You* are the light of the world" (John 9:5; Matthew 5:14). Paul recognizes, as Jesus said in John 9, that while Jesus was in the world he was the light of the world. Now that he has returned to the Father, Jesus has sent his Spirit to dwell in and empower his mystical body the Church so that "he who believes in me will also do the works that I do; and greater works than these will he do, because I go to the Father" (John 14:12). In other words, Paul, like Jesus, identifies the Church with Christ. This is not surprising since Paul's formative experience with Christ on the road to Damascus taught him to do exactly this. "Saul, Saul, why are you persecuting *me?*" asked the risen Christ. Strictly speaking, Saul was per-

secuting Christians, not Christ. Yet Jesus nonetheless in-
sisted that whatever Saul did to his Church he was doing to
Jesus.

Paul, taking this cue from Jesus, comes to understand
that the Church is therefore the sacramental presence of
Christ in the world. We do his work in the world. Our
sufferings are identified with his. We are glorified with
him. We participate in his "sacrificial offering." That is
why Paul can write, "Now I rejoice in my sufferings for
your sake, and in my flesh I complete what is lacking in
Christ's afflictions for the sake of his body, that is, the
Church" (Colossians 1:24). And because the Church shares
in the sufferings of Christ, she also shares in his glory and
in his work here on earth. This is why Paul writes to the
Ephesians:

> For this reason, because I have heard of your faith in
> the Lord Jesus and your love toward all the saints, I do
> not cease to give thanks for you, remembering you in my
> prayers, that the God of our Lord Jesus Christ, the Father
> of glory, may give you a spirit of wisdom and of reve-
> lation in the knowledge of him, having the eyes of your
> hearts enlightened, that you may know what is the hope to
> which he has called you, what are the riches of his glorious
> inheritance in the saints, and what is the immeasurable
> greatness of his power in us who believe, according to
> the working of his great might which he accomplished in
> Christ when he raised him from the dead and made him
> sit at his right hand in the heavenly places, far above all
> rule and authority and power and dominion, and above
> every name that is named, not only in this age but also in
> that which is to come; and he has put all things under his
> feet and has made him the head over all things for the

Church, which is his body, the fulness of him who fills all in all. (Ephesians 1:15–23)

This means that the moral sense of Scripture can be understood in yet another way: in addition to the direct didactic teaching of the Old and New Testaments and the actions of Christ, there is also the action of his Spirit-filled Church which offers us moral instruction as well. Thus, it is not only things done by Christ which offer us further insight into the moral sense of Scripture, it is also . . .

Things Done in Christ

One of the overlooked facts of the gospel is that while Jesus did many good and wonderful things, he did not by any stretch of the imagination do *everything*. Jesus tells us to clothe the naked. We have no record that he himself did so during his ministry. He tells us to visit those in prison. He himself did not do so (except in a certain ultimate sense when he permitted himself to be thrust into the heart of the prison population on the evening of his arrest, trial, and execution). He offered many good and worthy moral instructions which he himself did not have occasion to implement, not because he was a hypocrite, but because no human being can be everywhere and do everything. Rather, Jesus did good works as he had occasion but focused on his central mission: his death and resurrection for the salvation of the world.

This does not mean, however, that upon his ascension he went into retirement and now sits on the heavenly sofa watching videos all afternoon. On the contrary, Luke tells us in Acts 1:1 that the story of Jesus' earthly ministry related in his gospel is merely what Jesus "*began* to do and teach." The implication is clear: we ain't seen nothin' yet. In the book of Acts, Luke intends to show us how Jesus is continuing, guiding, and directing his work through the Church which is his Body. Like St. Teresa of Avila, Luke is acutely aware that Christ now has no hands or feet on earth but ours.

Therefore, we can gain still further insights into the moral sense of Scripture, not only from the words and deeds of Christ, but from the actions of his mystical body, the Church. The lives of the saints, like that of their Master, begin to become transparent to his light (albeit they still have the dirt and stain of sin blocking the view sometimes). And, as he promised, they go on to do things by the power of his Spirit which he himself did not undertake during his earthly ministry. That is why it is the Church led by the Spirit, not Jesus in the flesh, which has the principal task of bringing the gospel, not only to Judea and Samaria as Christ had done, but to the uttermost parts of the earth. That is why believers are described as performing signs and possessing spiritual gifts (in, for instance, Romans 12 and 1 Corinthians 12) which are not in evidence in the earthly ministry of Christ himself. Jesus, so far as we know, never prayed in tongues or gave interpretations of tongues, but members of his Church do by the power of his Spirit. Jesus, as a wandering itinerant preacher, had little occasion to exercise a gift of administration. But his Church has an ever-increasing opportunity and need to do so. In so doing, the Church continued to enflesh in its mystical body precisely the same divine life of the Holy Spirit that Jesus had incarnated in his human body. That is why Jesus himself said, "By this all men will know that you are my disciples, if you have love for one another" (John 13:35). Thus, like Jesus himself, his Church becomes a sign and sacrament of the love and grace of God for the world.

Things Which Signify Christ

But even this is not the extent of what we mean by the "moral sense" of Scripture. For as we have seen, in inspiring the Scriptures, God's Spirit saw to it that other sorts of pictures were provided to us not only after the advent of Christ, but well before. Some glimmer of this we have just seen in the curious circumstance of the Bread of Life coming into the world through the "House of Bread." But this is only scratching the surface. For, in fact, God providentially arranged that gobs of people, historic events, myths, poetry, fiction, and various forms of prophetic literature would present to our minds, hearts, and senses a rich and varied smorgasbord of images with which to illustrate the moral teachings of Christ.

How does this proceed? In various ways. One common example is to see the Temple referring, not merely to the literal Temple in Jerusalem, nor merely to the Church of Christ, but to our very bodies as well. Thus it is that Jesus will declare in John 2:19, "Destroy this temple, and in three days I will raise it up" and his Apostle John will specifically clarify that, "He spoke of the temple of his body" (John 2:21). With a cue like that, St. Paul will go on to compare the act of fornication with defiling the Temple itself.

Do you not know that your bodies are members of Christ? Shall I therefore take the members of Christ and make

them members of a prostitute? Never! Do you not know
that he who joins himself to a prostitute becomes one
body with her? For, as it is written, "The two shall become one." But he who is united to the Lord becomes one
spirit with him. Shun immorality. Every other sin which
a man commits is outside the body; but the immoral man
sins against his own body. Do you not know that your
body is a temple of the Holy Spirit within you, which you
have from God? (1 Corinthians 6:15–19)

The Temple, in other words, is understood in a *moral*
as well as an allegorical and literal sense. And the Church
after the apostles will not fail to pick up the ball and run
with this way of reading Scripture as well. So St. Ignatius
of Antioch tells the Philadelphians, "keep your bodies as if
they were God's temple." Likewise, The *Liber Graduum*,
from fourth-century Persia will teach that "the body is a
hidden temple, and the heart is a hidden altar." And, of
course, countless Christians since then have drawn the same
analogy.

Another very basic example of the moral sense of Scripture is a theme known to all readers of fairy tales: physical
ugliness bespeaks moral ugliness and physical beauty bespeaks moral beauty. Just as the physical ugliness of hundreds of witches and the physical beauty of hundreds of
lovely princesses in tales from all over the world has often
traditionally been used as an image of moral wickedness
and virtue, we should not be surprised to discover that
beauty and ugliness have also been used this way in Scripture. This is why Isaiah can write:

I will greatly rejoice in the LORD, my soul shall exult in
my God; for he has clothed me with the garments of salvation, he has covered me with the robe of righteousness,

as a bridegroom decks himself with a garland, and as a
bride adorns herself with her jewels. (Isaiah 61:10)

That is, the grizzled old prophet likens his own soul in
the presence of God to a beautiful, blushing bride standing
in the presence of her Beloved on her wedding day. Similarly, the writer of Proverbs will link destruction of the
soul with the ugly image of "the adulterous woman" while
holiness, greatness, and honor will be given to those who
seek after the beautiful woman called "Wisdom" (Proverbs
7–8). And in later Christian centuries, writers will see in
the ugliness of Leah and the beauty of Rachel (Jacob's two
wives) an image of sin and virtue.

Yet, lest we make too simple an assumption that physical beauty really equals moral beauty rather than merely
being an image of it, Scripture is also careful to point out
the other side of the coin:

Charm is deceitful, and beauty is vain,
    but a woman who fears the LORD is to be praised.
(Proverbs 31:30)

Indeed anyone who fears the LORD, no matter their looks,
class, race, or economic status, is to be praised according to
Scripture. Thus, we can read the story of God's selection
of David as yet another image of his love for our souls,
despite what human beings may think of us. Everyone else
may dismiss you, laboring under the illusion that the Sauls
of the world are cool because they are big hairy guys with
muscles. But it remains the case that God sees and loves
you, as he saw and loved David, not his skin color, bank
account, or height. Moreover, God can, through you as
through David, do wonderful and unexpected things such
as slaying "giants" of loneliness, anger, ignorance, greed,

prejudice, and fear which plague the people around you just as he used David to slay Goliath. Here, once again, Scripture can be read in its moral sense so that it provides a kind of iconography of the heart.

A third example of the moral sense of Scripture applied to the people and events of the Old Testament is the use that the New Testament and subsequent Christian writers make of the idea of physical struggle and warfare. As we saw earlier, the Old Testament is replete with imagery of warfare, battle, defeat, and victory — in particular, the image of the conquest of Canaan by Joshua and the Israelites. In this long campaign the promises made to Abraham and Moses begin to see fulfillment. The land, long a haunt of idols, uncleanness, and even child sacrifice, is at last to be made clean and fruitful by the children of Jacob led by their God. It is transformed from the land of Canaan to the Holy Land.

Such imagery provides fertile ground for the moral sense. And this is not lost on the biblical writers. The long struggle of the people of Israel (whose very name means "he who struggles with God") to be holy and faithful to the covenant frequently evokes images of battle, and this in turn can remind us of our own long, personal struggle against our own faults and failings. This is why the author of Proverbs writes:

> He who is slow to anger is better than the mighty,
> and he who rules his spirit than he who takes a city.
> (Proverbs 16:32)

And Jesus tells this parable:

> What king, going to encounter another king in war, will
> not sit down first and take counsel whether he is able

with ten thousand to meet him who comes against him
with twenty thousand? And if not, while the other is yet
a great way off, he sends an embassy and asks terms of
peace. So therefore, whoever of you does not renounce all
that he has cannot be my disciple. (Luke 14:31–33)

Isaiah also portrays the struggle for holiness with military imagery:

The LORD saw it, and it displeased him that there was no
justice. He saw that there was no man, and wondered that
there was no one to intervene; then his own arm brought
him victory, and his righteousness upheld him. He put on
righteousness as a breastplate, and a helmet of salvation
upon his head. (Isaiah 59:15–17)

And Paul sounds the same note in using martial imagery
to urge the Ephesians on in the struggle for holiness:

Finally, be strong in the Lord and in the strength of his
might. Put on the whole armor of God, that you may
be able to stand against the wiles of the devil. For we
are not contending against flesh and blood, but against
the principalities, against the powers, against the world
rulers of this present darkness, against the spiritual hosts
of wickedness in the heavenly places. Therefore take the
whole armor of God, that you may be able to withstand
in the evil day, and having done all, to stand. Stand therefore, having girded your loins with truth, and having put
on the breastplate of righteousness, and having shod your
feet with the equipment of the gospel of peace; besides
all these, taking the shield of faith, with which you can
quench all the flaming darts of the evil one. And take the
helmet of salvation, and the sword of the Spirit, which is
the word of God. (Ephesians 6:10–17)

In short, one can read the stories of battle in the Old Testament literally (about the military triumphs of Israel), allegorically (about the triumph of Christ over Satan), or in view of the moral sense (seeing the triumph of grace over sin, virtue over vice, and life over death). That is why St. Peter can urge us to "abstain from the passions of the flesh that make war against your soul" (1 Peter 2:11). And it is why Church Fathers such as Pope St. Leo the Great (in *The Binding of the Strong Man*) can, for instance, understand the seven nations driven out of Canaan by Joshua (whose name in Hebrew is the same as Jesus: Y'shua) as an image of the seven deadly sins driven out of the soul by Christ who leads us to conquer sin and establish holiness.

A Final Caveat about the Moral Sense

One advantage of reading Scripture in this way is that it helps us to derive benefit from certain difficult passages (particularly in the Old Testament) which, in their literal sense, are very hard for moderns to receive. C. S. Lewis, for instance, writes:

> I can use even the horrible passage in [Psalm] 137 about dashing the Babylonian babies against the stones. I know things in the inner world which are like babies; the infantile beginnings of small indulgences, small resentments, which may one day become dipsomania or settled hatred, but which woo us and wheedle us with special pleadings and seems so tiny, so helpless that in resisting them we feel we are being cruel to animals. They begin whimpering to us "I don't ask much, but", or "I had at least hoped", or "You owe yourself *some* consideration". Against all such

pretty infants (the dears have such winning ways) the advice of the psalm is the best. Knock the little bastards' brains out. And "blessed" is he who can, for it's easier said than done.[2]

But, of course, we can only read Scripture in this way if we remain honest about the fact that the literal sense of Scripture continues to hold priority. And this leaves us with a very big problem, particularly with respect to the sometimes terrible violence and cruelty recorded in the Old Testament, but also with respect to other questions such as polygamy or the nearly nonexistent belief in the afterlife evidenced in some Old Testament books. What do we do about what appear to be such major disconnects between the Old and New Testaments? It is often temptingly easy to embrace one of the following extremely simple solutions to the problem:

Simple Solution No. 1 is the one settled on by most modern people. It is to simply deny the inspired character of those texts of Scripture we happen to find distasteful or troubling. And so we often find flat denials that God inspired the accounts of the conquest of Canaan. The difficulty with this is that Simple Solution No. 1, though easy, is dishonest (at least from a Christian perspective) because it fundamentally rejects what Christ and his Church fundamentally assert is true: that "*all* scripture is inspired", not just the bits we happen to like (2 Timothy 3:16).

Solution No. 2 is to explain away the literal sense of Scripture by allowing some symbolic reading of it to predominate. Now it is legitimate to read Psalm 137 in the moral sense as referring to ruthlessly destroying our own

---

[2] Lewis, *Reflections on the Psalms*, p. 136.

sins and vices, as Lewis does above. However, it would not have been legitimate for Lewis to pretend that Psalm 137 was not written in part to praise an act of vengeance fundamentally incompatible with the teaching of Christ. (Lewis, being both honest and intelligent, does not do this; which is why he frankly acknowledges the problem of the psalm as asserting a "horrible" moral vision.) To adopt Simple Solution No. 2 is dishonest because, as we have seen, the Church clearly teaches that the literal sense of Scripture (i.e. what the human author of Scripture really meant to say) must take priority over any other sense of Scripture.

Solution No. 3 (not as popular but still acceptable to certain hard-as-nails kinds of Christians) is to simply affirm wholesale all Old Testament morality from hamstringing horses to stoning rebellious adolescents to butchering Canaanite babies as "the will of God." But this too is problematic given the Christian demand for radical charity and forgiveness of enemies and the enormous contrast between this demand and the bloodthirsty behavior we so often find in the Old Testament.

So we seem to be faced with an insoluble problem: inspired Scripture that apparently advocates two completely irreconcilable kinds of morality. What do we do?

The first thing is to make no rash moves. We must be very cautious in searching through Scripture for its "moral sense" because the morality taught by Scripture is not a *static* thing. As with the revelation of the coming Messiah himself, so the revelation of a fully human and fully divine morality is, in fact, an unfolding thing. It is therefore a grave mistake to seize on isolated texts of the Old Testament and declare "The Bible" approves wars of extermination, divorce and disbelief in the afterlife. "The Bible" is not that simple because it is the record of an inspired revelation that did not take place in the wink of an eye, but over the course of centuries.

Think of a human embryo. At one point it has a tail. But the adult human doesn't. Is it really accurate to say humans are creatures with tails? No, even though at one stage in the womb we were. The same principle applies here. Revelation progressed like a developing embryo from the Old Testament to the New. God permitted divorce under the Mosaic Covenant, for instance. Yet Jesus would later make clear that this was a *permission*, not "God's will" (Mark 10:5). Similarly, God condescended to the practice of the culture to which he first revealed himself when he "stooped down" and submitted himself to the practice of "cutting a covenant" with Abraham by passing between the severed halves of the animal carcasses (Genesis 15). But though God blessed forms of sacrifice and covenant which were perfectly acceptable in Abraham's day, his ultimate goal was always to lead us to the final and full sacrifice and covenant offered by Christ. In the same way, there were moral, ethical and philosophical insights in Abraham's day which were good as far as they went, but they have since been fulfilled and completed by the final and full revelation offered by Christ.

And so, Abraham, Moses, and David knew in a rough and ready way certain basic moral precepts: as that you should love your neighbor and also fight for justice. Not surprisingly, this often meant killing your neighbor when he was unjust, an experience we in our own century are not wholly unfamiliar with when our neighbor was a Nazi. But in an ancient Near Eastern culture that has no concept of the human person (as no culture had in antiquity) there was at first no possibility of appealing to the dignity of each human person nor of trying to speak about individual guilt or innocence, even to Abraham, Moses, and David. In Judaism, the idea of personal, individual responsibility for sin is a very late development. The prophet Ezekiel (who is writing during the Babylonian Exile around 600 B.C.) only starts to hint at it when he says that the son should not be held guilty for the sin of the father (Ezekiel 18:1–24). In earlier Israelite religion, such a concept was scarcely there at all. And so, people were understood in ancient Near Eastern culture to be "guilty" of being an Amorite or a Canaanite and fine distinctions were not made about personal responsibility for the sins of their people, nor could they be conceived of even if God had tried to reveal them. In an era where Israel was fighting for its life, fine philosophical distinctions did not have time to be made. So "Canaanites" — man, woman and child — were butchered because that was the best that could be done given the assumptions of the culture.

Notably, however, this changes as revelation progresses. By the time of Ezra and Nehemiah, Israel will still take a dismissive approach to the Samaritans as a people yet they will not understand themselves to have divine permission to exterminate them, despite the fact that they are regarded as a corrupt nation by the Jews. Jesus, going still further, will make distinctions between "good Samaritans" and "bad Israelites" (Luke 10:29–37). And the later Church will go further yet (following Christ's lead), and invent the concept of "the person" which we all use today.

This same principle of unfolding revelation is seen in the development of the Jewish understanding of the afterlife. So, for instance, Ecclesiastes tells us that "life is vanity" and speaks in a despairing tone about the futility of earthly existence. That is because Ecclesiastes is unaware of the resurrection of the Body which was not fully revealed until later. He is right as far as he goes. Earthly life *is* futile. He simply doesn't (and can't) go far enough without further revelation.

Similarly, many Old Testament figures have no qualms about nursing grudges against enemies and murdering them when given the chance (1 Kings 2:1–9). This is not because they know *nothing* of fully revealed morality, but because they only know *part* of it: the part about justice, not mercy. And it was because they only knew part of it that Jesus was obliged to say:

> You have heard that it was said, 'You shall love your neighbor and hate your enemy.' But I say to you, Love your enemies and pray for those who persecute you, so that you may be sons of your Father who is in heaven; for he makes his sun rise on the evil and on the good, and sends rain on the just and on the unjust. For if you love those who love you, what reward have you? Do not even the tax collectors do the same? And if you salute only your brethren, what more are you doing than others? Do not even the Gentiles do the same? You, therefore, must be perfect, as your heavenly Father is perfect. (Matthew 5:43–48)

Bottom line: Much Old Testament morality and theology regarding war, marriage, the afterlife, the demand for justice and so forth is true as far as it goes, but often the author has not yet gone far enough because the Holy Spirit has not yet revealed it. In the Old Testament, the Chosen People were not yet the recipients of full revelation. That full revelation was Jesus Christ, who definitively clarified all that went before and fulfilled what was not complete. This is the idea of the development of doctrine. We understand this idea completely when we contemplate our own children. There are things we permit of (and punishments we inflict on) three-year-olds that are appropriate for their stage of development which would be absurd to permit of (or inflict on) a twenty-year-old.

Which takes us to one of the central problems of the Old Testament. Namely, that it is a revelation whereby a transcendent God of all perfection was obliged to plunge into the cesspool of a fallen race and start his work of redemption *somewhere*. That is, it is revelation which took place "in time and on earth" and not in some cloud-cuckoo land of myth. Therefore, it is a revelation which begins in the real, concrete circumstances of a given culture and people — a people who, like all others of the time, were barbarians. This being so, God was obliged to work through and with a people with faults, idiosyncrasies, blind spots and errors resulting from their being as fallen as the rest of the human race. Yet he was obliged to do so, not in order to ratify the Fall, but in order to mend it. This meant, as all teachers know, making allowances for the weaknesses of the student till the student matured further. It meant facing the fact that the world into which Israel marched out of Egypt was a *real* world, not an ideal one, and that facing that world (a world where idolatry, wars of extermination, child sacrifice, polygamy, and other such complicating features were the norm for all participants) would mean a long, hard road to building a civilization and an even longer road to the day when the human race was ready to hear the (at the time) unimaginable truth of Christ.

Thus, to complain that God did not immediately intro-

duce the full moral and ethical teaching of Christ into the
diet of Israel is like complaining that a parent does not
immediately force feed a baby sirloin steak and a bottle of
wine. It is like finding fault with a kindergarten teacher
for neglecting to introduce the kidlets to the inner mysteries of integral calculus, algebra and quantum physics. As
Christ taught of divorce, so it may be said of many of the
moral imperfections permitted in the Old Testament: "For
your hardness of heart he wrote you this commandment"
(Mark 10:5). It was not that God changed from the Old
Testament to the New. It was that *we* had to grow up
enough to bear the full truth about him and his demands
on us. Our eyes had to get used to the Light.

And that means two things:

First, in seeking the moral sense of Scripture, we as
Christians must always read it in light of the fullness of
the revelation which Christ has given.

Second, if God is best understood in the Old Testament
as "stooping down" to our level and teaching us till we
would be "big enough" to receive the fullness of his revelation in Christ, we must also realize that, since Christ has
come, God is not so much concerned to bend down to our
level, as to lift us up to his.[3] It is with this reality in mind
that we look at the last of the four senses of Scripture: the
anagogical sense.

---

[3] For examples of this idea of God's "bending down" and "lifting up"
the human race in the Fathers of the Church, see Stephen D. Benin,
*The Footprints of God: Divine Accommodation in Jewish and Christian
Thought* (SUNY Series in Judaica: Hermeneutics, Mysticism, and Religion), (New York: State University of New York Press, July 1993).

9

The Anagogical Sense of Scripture

He will come again in glory to judge the living and the dead and his kingdom will have no end.

— Nicene Creed

As was noted earlier in this book, the story of our creation, redemption, and salvation is, among other things, a *story* with a beginning, middle, and end. The beginning and middle we have considered. But Scripture and the Church also teach us that we will not be living in the middle of the story forever. History is *going* somewhere and will reach a final consummation in what are known as the Four Last Things: Death, Judgment, Heaven, and Hell.

What We Were Made for and Where We're Going

Way back in our discussion of the covenant with Adam we noted that the primordial tasks of the human race were marriage, fruitfulness, rule, work, and worship. What we have discovered since then is that all of these tasks have been redeemed by Christ and, since Jesus remains human forever and ascended to heaven, they are *raised* by Jesus Christ to a transcendent level. He is the Groom and his Church is the Bride. He is the Vine who causes us to "bear much fruit" (John 15:5). He is "the head of all rule and authority" (Colossians 2:10). He is the one who accomplishes God's work (John 4:34). And he is one who offers the perfect worship to the Father because he is the beloved Son (Matthew 3:17).

This "raising" of the covenant with Adam to this cosmic and transcendent level has astonishing implications for us. For it means that the ultimate goal of human life is not found in God's bending down to earth but in his raising us up to Heaven. God became a participant in human nature not for its own sake, but so that *we* could become "participants in the *divine* nature" (2 Peter 1:4). Everything that was hinted at in the Garden of Eden will one day be ours to a degree and dimension which "eye has not seen, nor ear heard" (1 Corinthians 2:9). Even more, in the giddy paradox of divine generosity, we have been granted gifts in Christ greater than those we possessed before the Fall. This is why the Church sings in the Easter liturgy, "O happy fault! O necessary sin of Adam that gained for us so great a salvation." The Fall remains as evil and tragic as ever, but God's choice to become human and to eternally join his deity to our humanity in Christ exalts humankind to a staggering degree.

Turning the World Upside-down

It also turns things on their heads in unexpected ways. We begin to discover, for example, that some of our com-

fortable commonplaces are not at all what we thought.
Take the idea of fatherhood. Most of us, used to the idea
that God stoops down to our level to reveal himself, will
naturally assume that when God reveals himself as "Father" to us he is doing so because he is borrowing the image
of fatherhood from our vocabulary. It is just here, however, the Scriptures set things topsy-turvy. For Paul tells
us (Ephesians 3:14–15) not that God derives the image of
fatherhood from us, but that "every fatherhood, in Heaven
and on earth, takes its name" from God the Father. That
is, we are made in *his* image, not he in ours. We get the
idea of fatherhood from *him*, not he from us.

Likewise, when it really begins to dawn on us that the
man Christ Jesus is also the God who has existed from all
eternity we begin to realize that he is not the Johnny-come-
lately in history but the one who exists before and beyond
all worlds and all history. In other words, he did not get the
idea of sacrificial death from watching the lambs slaugh-
tered at Passover. Rather, Israel's practice of sacrifice was
revealed to them *by him* on Mt. Sinai as a dim foreshadow
of his own self-sacrifice as the true "Lamb of God" (John
1:29). That is why the author of Hebrews writes of the
Jewish priests serving in the Temple at Jerusalem:

> They serve a copy and shadow of the heavenly sanctuary;
> for when Moses was about to erect the tent, he was in-
> structed by God, saying, "See that you make everything
> according to the pattern which was shown you on the
> mountain." (Hebrews 8:5)

In other words, the earthly worship of God that went
on in the tabernacle and in the Temple was only an image
of the true worship that is offered by the Son to the Fa-

ther in heaven. In the Old Testament, God "bent down" and made Israel participants in that worship by means of a "copy and shadow of the heavenly sanctuary" just as an earthly father might give his child a picture of some difficult-to-grasp adult reality in order to prepare that child for later life. In the same way, the various furniture and liturgical rites of ancient Israel were revealed in order to prepare Israel for the heavenly realities they signified.

Raised up with Christ

But the preparation was not to last forever. In the New Testament God stops bending down and begins to lift up. This "lifting up" of humanity takes place (as the death and resurrection of humanity took place) first and foremost in the person of the Son of Man who *is* Humanity, at his ascension. But the Church is expected to follow him and, in its worship, is understood to participate in the worship Christ offers the Father in the heavenly Throne Room. That is why the book of Hebrews speaks of our confidently approaching the "throne of grace" (Hebrews 4:16) and it is why, in the book of Revelation, we see this explicitly depicted when the voice from Heaven speaks to the author commanding, "*Come up hither*, and I will show you what must take place after this" (Revelation 4:1). The author of Revelation (and, by implication, we his readers) may now go *up*, God need not come down to us. The Way is open. And in going up, we find ourselves participating in the heavenly worship. For a major point of Revelation is that the various acts of worship we engage in during this life are not something we do to occupy our time until we get to Heaven and get a break. Rather, our earthly acts of worship are, in fact, a participation in (and preparation for) the eternal act of worship in which the Son offers himself and all creation to the Father by the Spirit. In short, worship is not our idea. It is God's. When we worship, we are being taken up into the never-ending life of love and self offering between the three Persons of the Blessed Trinity and we are being slowly conformed to the image of Christ. Thus the picture of worship in the book of Revelation is not one which implies that heavenly life is a sort of dim shadow of earth but rather that our worship is done (if it is done rightly at all) "on earth *as it is in heaven.*"

This is why Revelation can speak of the coming of Christ's kingdom and call it the "new Jerusalem" (Revelation 21:10). For the writer of Revelation is aware of a fourth sense of Scripture. He recognizes that Jerusalem can be understood not only in a literal sense (i.e., as a physical city in Judea), an allegorical sense (i.e., as an image of the Church) and a moral sense (i.e., as an image of the soul), but also in an anagogical sense (that is, in a sense which speaks of our final destiny). And so, we find, in this instance, Jerusalem here being used to depict our heavenly destiny.

It is worth noting that Scripture, when it sees in Jerusalem an icon of heavenly reality, is necessarily seeing Heaven as fundamentally *social*. The human race may have begun in a quiet garden, but it is emphatically destined for a *city*. Indeed, Revelation goes out of its way to portray Heaven neither as a dewy Elysian field nor as a mystic cave where the solitary saint goes to contemplate the face of God far from the madding crowd, nor as a "state of mind." On the contrary, the very suggestion that Heaven is a subjective "state of mind" would elicit from the author of Revelation the same reaction that it elicits from the glorious spirit of George Macdonald in C. S. Lewis' *The Great Divorce*:

> "Hush," said he sternly. "Do not blaspheme. Hell is a state of mind — ye never said a truer word. And every state of mind, left to itself, every shutting up of the creature within the dungeon of its own mind — is, in the end, Hell. But Heaven is not a state of mind. Heaven is reality itself."[1]

And so, because it is fully real and therefore utterly *public*, Heaven is portrayed in Revelation as a place of teeming throngs, bustle and even ferment. Its population is enormous ("a great multitude which no man could number, from every nation, from all tribes and peoples and tongues, standing before the throne and before the Lamb, clothed in white robes, with palm branches in their hands, and crying out with a loud voice, 'Salvation belongs to our God who sits upon the throne, and to the Lamb!'" [Revelation 7:9–10]). Moreover, the knowledge of the God who is worshiped there is *public* and *common*, not intricate, mysterious, esoteric and hidden from the multitude. It is "plain as daylight" to everybody. That is why the author of Revelation tells us "they shall see his face, and his name shall be on their foreheads. And night shall be no more; they need no light of lamp or sun, for the Lord God will be their light, and they shall reign for ever and ever" (Revelation 22:4–5). Further, the saints in glory (as well as the angels, archangels, and entire company of heaven) are conscious not only of God, but of each other and of matters on earth. They behave exactly as though Paul knew what

---

[1] C. S. Lewis, *The Great Divorce* (Macmillan: New York, 1973), p. 69.

he was talking about when he emphasized to the Romans that they were members, not only of Christ, but of "one another" (Romans 12:5).

In addition to the way in which Scripture sees Jerusalem as a sign of heaven's sociableness, it is also worth noting that Scripture sees in the image of *royalty* another sign of our heavenly destiny. As we just saw, Scripture speaks of the saints in Heaven "reigning" for ever and ever with Christ. Paul speaks of the same thing, telling the Corinthians, "Already you are filled! Already you have become rich! Without us you have become kings! And would that you did reign, so that we might share the rule with you!" (1 Corinthians 4:8). Similarly, Paul declares at the end of his life, "Henceforth there is laid up for me the crown of righteousness, which the Lord, the righteous judge, will award to me on that Day, and not only to me but also to all who have loved his appearing" (2 Timothy 4:8). In other words, Scripture affirms not only that we are with Christ and with each other in Heaven, but that we shall share in his "reign" and therefore in his power and authority. It is not surprising, therefore, that Scripture portrays the saints as wearing crowns and yet, also, that those same saints offer those crowns back to God in homage (Revelation 4:10). Nor is it strange that the New Testament, as we have seen, should look backward through Old Testament history and understand the crown and kingdom of David to refer, not to an endless political reign, but to the kingdom of Messiah as promised in Psalm 110. And so, the writer to the Hebrews has no difficulty reading a royal wedding ode like Psalm 45 (which was originally written for one of the Davidic Kings on his wedding day) and using the anagogical sense of Scripture to see in it a reference to the ultimate Son of David — Messiah — entering into his heavenly reign.

The Wedding Feast of the Lamb

Why does the writer of Hebrews have no difficulty doing this? Because he recognizes that marriage is yet another occasion where the revelation of Christ has turned the world upside down. Just as our idea of fatherhood actually comes from God the Father, our idea of sacrifice comes from the sacrifice of the Lamb of God who is Jesus, and our idea of worship is modeled on the heavenly worship offered through all eternity, so our idea of *marriage* is actually a mere dim reflection of the heavenly Groom who is Christ and his Bride, the Church. That is exactly why St. Paul writes:

> Be subject to one another out of reverence for Christ. Wives, be subject to your husbands, as to the Lord. For the husband is the head of the wife as Christ is the head of the Church, his body, and is himself its Savior. As the Church is subject to Christ, so let wives also be subject in everything to their husbands. Husbands, love your wives, as Christ loved the Church and gave himself up for her, that he might sanctify her, having cleansed her by the washing of water with the word, that he might present the Church to himself in splendor, without spot or wrinkle or any such thing, that she might be holy and without blemish. Even so husbands should love their wives as their own bodies. He who loves his wife loves himself. For no man ever hates his own flesh, but nourishes and cherishes it, as Christ does the Church, because we are members of his body. "For this reason a man shall leave his father and mother and be joined to his wife, and the two shall become one flesh." This mystery is a profound one, and I am saying that it refers to Christ and the Church. (Ephesians 5:21–32)

Many modern readers make a mistake of zeroing in the passage about wives being subject to their husbands as the be all and end all of this passage. This is, however, to ignore the whole context. The reality is that Paul calls husbands and wives to "be subject to *one another* out of reverence for Christ." And that is because the whole mystery of mutual self-giving between husband and wife refers us, not to the husband and wife, but "to Christ and the Church." For, as we saw earlier, the Church is the Bride of the last Adam as Eve was the bride of the first Adam. We are "one flesh" with Christ as Eve was one flesh with Adam. Not surprisingly then, the author of Revelation has another name for the "new Jerusalem." He calls it the "Bride" (Revelation 21:9). And he gets the idea from Jesus who likewise compares Heaven to a wedding banquet (Matthew 22:1–14).

To speak of bride and groom as "one flesh" is to say, among other things, that the fortunes of the one are bound up with the fortunes of the other. This means, as we have seen, that Jesus reckons both the evil and the good done to his Church as having been done to him. That is why he tells the parable of the sheep and the goats (Matthew 25:31–46) and that is why he rebukes the persecuting Saul of Tarsus with the words, "Saul, Saul, why are you persecuting *me*?" (Acts 9:4). What is done to the least of his brethren is done to him.

On the other hand, the destiny of Jesus becomes the destiny of his Bride. We are to be "like him" (1 John 3:2). That means more than a mere demand to imitate his moral teachings or character (as if that were a small thing!). It means, as we have seen, that we are to share in his divine sonship and in his very life. That is why Paul writes:

When we cry, "Abba! Father!" it is the Spirit himself bearing witness with our spirit that we are children of God, and if children, then heirs, heirs of God and fellow heirs with Christ, provided we suffer with him in order that we may also be glorified with him. (Romans 8:15–17)

The Christian's Shared Destiny with Christ

Our destiny, then, is bound up with Christ's. This means, in the most childlike terms, that because Jesus went to Heaven, those in union with him will too. But there is more, and it is something comfortable Americans like us do not like to hear. Namely, as George Macdonald said, "the Son of God suffered unto the death, not that men might not suffer, but that their sufferings might be like His."[2] In short, we don't share *only* in his glory. Rather, as Jesus shares in our sufferings so we share in his. Both the Church and its individual members are bound to participate, not only in his resurrection, but in his cross. That is why Jesus himself says,

If the world hates you, know that it has hated me before it hated you. If you were of the world, the world would love its own; but because you are not of the world, but I chose you out of the world, therefore the world hates you. Remember the word that I said to you, "A servant is not greater than his master." If they persecuted me, they will persecute you; if they kept my word, they will keep yours also. (John 15:18–20)

---

[2] George Macdonald, *Unspoken Sermons. First Series.*

Individually, the members of the Church experience this frequently. Disciples of Christ suffer and even die for Christ all over the world to this day. And, in our daily lives, all Christians experience various trials and tribulations ranging from illness to divorce to family difficulties to the inevitable death that we all must sooner or later endure. In all this, we are called to deny ourselves, take up our cross daily and follow Christ (Matthew 16:24).

The Church's Shared Destiny with Christ

However, what some people are starting to forget is that what is true of Christ and of his individual followers is also true of the Church as a whole. Some people dream of a happy earthly destiny for the Church of Christ. They hope that, as the Church spreads out across the world, then perhaps little by little and bit by bit, every day in every way, the world will get better until the Kingdom of Heaven comes in the Great Rosy Dawn. Others, most notably in this century, have tried to tinker together a man-made heavenly kingdom and have given it names like National Socialism, Communism, Maoism, Hedonism, Materialism, the Playboy Philosophy, the Triumph of Reason, etc. All these schemes share in the common hope of achieving the happiness of the resurrection without having to go to the trouble of dying. Several of the more energetic forms have, however, taken great trouble to kill on a massive scale. This "counterfeit messianism" is precisely what the Church warns us against. Indeed, the unbroken tradition of the Church holds precisely that "[b]efore Christ's second coming the Church must pass through a final trial that will shake the faith of many believers. The persecution that accompanies her pilgrimage on earth will unveil the 'mystery of iniquity' in the form of a religious deception offering men an apparent solution to their problems at the price of apostasy from the truth. The supreme religious deception is that of the Antichrist, the pseudo-messianism by which man glorifies himself in place of God and of his Messiah come in the flesh" (*CCC*, no. 675). The Church as a whole, like her members and like her Lord, will not get to take a shortcut. She too must pass through death to resurrection.

Here again, we find the image of Jerusalem being thrust at us by the gospel writers and endowed with the anagogical sense. In Matthew 24, for instance, the prophecies of Jesus concerning the destruction of Jerusalem by the Romans in 70 A.D. and his prophecies concerning his coming at the end of time are almost seamlessly intermingled (something that has caused endless puzzlement for Bible students as well as guaranteeing job security for biblical scholars all over the world). Why do the gospel writers mix these prophecies together? Because, in a very real sense, the gospel writers see them as referring to nearly the same thing. This does not mean the gospel writers fancy that the world came to an end in 70 A.D. with the sack of Jerusalem. Rather, it means that the "death" Jerusalem suffered when the Temple was destroyed is an image of the death Jesus suffered in the temple of his body *and* an image of the death the Body of Christ will one day undergo in the final climactic battle between light and darkness before the return of Christ. In the words of the *Catechism of the Catholic Church* (no. 677):

The Church will enter the glory of the kingdom only
through this final Passover, when she will follow her
Lord in his death and Resurrection. The kingdom will
be fulfilled, then, not by a historic triumph of the Church
through a progressive ascendancy, but only by God's victory over the final unleashing of evil, which will cause his
Bride to come down from heaven. God's triumph over
the revolt of evil will take the form of the Last Judgment
after the final cosmic upheaval of this passing world.

Hell: The Refusal of Our Destiny in Christ

In short, the gospel writers, following their Master, see in
the sufferings of Jerusalem something of the mystery of the
cross just as they see in the exaltation of Jerusalem something of the mystery of Easter and of our glorious heavenly destiny. Similarly, both the gospel writers and Jesus
use the literal valley of Ennom, southwest of Jerusalem as
an image of hell (Matthew 5:22). The literal place (called
"Gehenna") had been the scene of idolatry and afterwards
became a place to burn garbage. But it was given an anagogical significance by Jesus to refer to the place where
souls could wind up on the garbage heap if they refuse his
grace.

The Communion of Saints:
Our Mutual Destiny in Christ

But the thought of hell by no means dominates in the
New Testament. The New Testament writers are too inspired by hope for that to be the case. Thus, the New Testament writers, compelled by the vision of heavenly glory

offered them by the risen Christ, seize on many Old Testament figures and scenes as references to our heavenly destiny. And so, the letter to the Hebrews urges us to press on to our "great reward" (Hebrews 10:35) and then refers us to a long list of Old Testament worthies who "desire a better country, that is, a heavenly one" and for whom God has "prepared . . . a city" (Hebrews 11:16). In these figures — Abel who is dead yet who speaks, Noah who passed through the waters of death to life, Abraham who offered his son Isaac up in sacrifice and received him back alive, Joseph who went into the pit and was raised up to glory, Israel who went into slavery and passed through the waters of death into the Promised Land, as well as many others — we see a myriad of little Easter mysteries throughout the history of Israel repeating again and again: both shadows of the cross and rumors of glory. When we look at them we see something of what we ourselves are approaching. For we have

> come to Mount Zion and to the city of the living God, the heavenly Jerusalem, and to innumerable angels in festal gathering, and to the assembly of the first-born who are enrolled in heaven, and to a judge who is God of all, and to the spirits of just men made perfect, and to Jesus, the mediator of a new covenant, and to the sprinkled blood that speaks more graciously than the blood of Abel. (Hebrews 12:22–24)

But (such is the sociableness of the New Jerusalem) we do not merely look at the saints. They look at us. That is why the writer of Hebrews tells us that we are surrounded by a "cloud of witnesses" who watch our progress toward the new Jerusalem like a giant crowd watches a runner in a race (Hebrews 12:1). And the race we run is modeled on the race run by Jesus "who for the joy that was set before him endured the cross, despising the shame, and is seated at the right hand of the throne of God" (Hebrews 12:2).

Purgatory: Prelude to Heaven

This means more than dying a "cross death." It also means living a "cross life." It means that there is a way of sanctity we must walk, a path we must take that the Master has taken before us. It means that salvation is both an event (as birth is an event), a process (as growing up is a process) and a consummation (as mature adult love in marriage is a consummation). That process involves pain for us as it involved pain for Christ, but it is pain unto life, not suffering unto damnation. That is why St. Paul tells us that "we rejoice in our sufferings, knowing that suffering produces endurance, and endurance produces character, and character produces hope, and hope does not disappoint us, because God's love has been poured into our hearts through the Holy Spirit which has been given to us" (Romans 5:3–5). In Paul's thought, eternal life is no more guaranteed by a single act of faith long ago than natural life is guaranteed by a single breath at birth. We must keep breathing. Or, to use the biblical image, we must "abide" or "remain" in Christ (John 15:1–11). Faith means you *stay*, even when it hurts. For even the hurt is part of the blessing in Christ.

This is also why the letter to the Hebrews insists that our sufferings as Christians are not a sign of rejection, but a sign that we are truly children of God. He writes:

> "My son, do not regard lightly the discipline of the Lord, nor lose courage when you are punished by him. For the Lord disciplines him whom he loves, and chastises every

son whom he receives." It is for discipline that you have to endure. God is treating you as sons; for what son is there whom his father does not discipline? If you are left without discipline, in which all have participated, then you are illegitimate children and not sons. Besides this, we have had earthly fathers to discipline us and we respected them. Shall we not much more be subject to the Father of spirits and live? For they disciplined us for a short time at their pleasure, but he disciplines us for our good, that we may share his holiness. For the moment all discipline seems painful rather than pleasant; later it yields the peaceful fruit of righteousness to those who have been trained by it. (Hebrews 12:5–11)

In all this, pain (which all of us must suffer whether we are Christian or not) is not *wasted*. Rather, it is, like all things in Christ, "taken up" and made part of our glory. This is not to say that pain, evil, and injustice are good. The sins of the human race that put the sinless Jesus on the cross, the evils and injustices that plague our world, the lousy things we ourselves have done remain sinful, evil, unjust and plain lousy. But they are *redeemed*. They are not the last word. They become, in delicious triumph, the unwilling servants of the good they tried to thwart. And we, in our patient endurance of this cleansing or purgative work of God, become more like his Son. That is, by the grace of God we do not merely *go* to heaven, we are slowly *made heavenly* so that we will enjoy it and be "fit" for it once we're there.

This process begins on earth and takes as long as it takes. For we are not merely to be forgiven by Christ, we are to be perfected in his image (a fact recognized whenever a Christian says, "Please be patient. God is not finished with me yet" and emphatically underscored by Paul in Philippians 3:12–14 and John in 1 John 3:2–3). This process of being conformed to the image of Christ (cf. Romans 8:29) extends until that point when we have died to ourselves and come alive to God so completely that we are purged of all sin by his grace (a point seldom reached by most of us in this life). If that process is *not* finished when we die, it is completed by God's relentless love in and for us after death (since, "nothing unclean shall enter" Heaven [Revelation 21:27]). This process, called "Purgatory" is therefore a thing which starts in this life with the purging of our sins and selfishness every day as we "take up our cross and follow" Jesus (cf. Matthew 16:24). It is a thing which ends with our complete transformation into the likeness of Christ either in this life or after death. If it *is* completed after death (as is typically the case for most people since most of us do not attain complete sanctity in this life), this does not make it a "second chance" for those who did not accept God's grace in this life. Rather, Purgatory is the *completion* of the work of grace which began in this life. It is the final polish on the image of Christ God has spent a lifetime sculpting in our souls.

This, once again, is something we can see pre-figured in Scripture in various places. We noted it, for example, in the long period of trial David had to undergo even after his prayer of contrition. Indeed, the long period of trial was the answer to his prayer for it was the way in which God not only forgave him, but changed him.

Likewise, we saw how the furnace of affliction through which Moses passed in his struggles with the people of Israel made him, all unaware, assume an attitude of intercessory prayer like Christ's. And that attitude did not wear off. For some 1,300 years later we find a thoroughly heavenly Moses speaking with the incarnate God on the Mount of Transfiguration and still very concerned about God and his people (Matthew 17:1–8). So, for that matter, are the citizens of Heaven in the book of Revelation, whose principal concern after the worship of God is the final coming of the kingdom of Heaven to earth.

This means that the process of being made heavenly, in Paul's understanding, means more than merely our personal relationship with Jesus. Sometimes, as we see from Hebrews 12:5–11 above, our sharing in the cross of Christ involves suffering so as to be cleansed of our own sin and filled with his life. But at other times our suffering is an even deeper share in the cross of Christ and is borne, not for our own sake but, like Christ's, for the sake of others. That is why Paul writes:

> Now I rejoice in my sufferings for your sake, and in my flesh I complete what is lacking in Christ's afflictions for the sake of his body, that is, the church. (Colossians 1:24)

Paul does not mean that Jesus did not do enough on the cross. Rather, he means that it is the glory of the Christian to participate in the outworking of Christ's act of redemptive suffering throughout the course of history. And the Christian, reading his Bible, recognizes that our participation in Christ's suffering (and therefore our entry into the life of heavenly glory) is something that has, in one sense, been going on since the dawn of time. That is exactly why Hebrews 11 can see in the sufferings and ultimate glory of Old Testament saints a whole panoply of images foretelling our own destiny, if we are but faithful as they were.

For Purgatory, as we have noted, shall not last forever

any more than courtship between lovers shall forever postpone the wedding. That is the promise of Scripture. God means to have us for his own. And not merely to have us as a man might own a statue, but to have us as the Lover has his Beloved. Even more shockingly, we are to have him as the Beloved has her Lover. This is precisely why St. Bernard of Clairvaux sees so much of our destiny depicted in the intense love poetry of the Song of Songs. We are not merely to be "accepted." We are to be *changed*, rendered glorious right down to the very core of our being. (1 Corinthians 15:51–52) To merely accept us yet not change us is to "cleanse the outside of the cup and of the plate" yet to leave the inside full of extortion and rapacity. It was precisely this contradiction that Jesus repudiated in no uncertain terms. Therefore, in the hope of Heaven and in the hope of being made heavenly, we can rest in the faith that Jesus himself will do what he himself demands and "cleanse the inside of the cup and of the plate, that the outside also may be clean" (Matthew 23:25–26). We shall not only be *where* the risen Christ is, we shall, in a manner befitting us as creatures, share in *what* the risen Christ is.

Heaven: Eternal Joy

Sharing in what the risen Christ is amounts to nothing less than a share in absolute, ecstatic, never-ending joy. In the grace and power of Christ, we begin to experience even in this life the capacity to love where we could not love before, to hope where previously we had only despair, to have faith where hitherto we had known only doubt. Moreover, we begin to recognize that it is not empty philosophy or mere poetic theologizing to see in our neighbor an immense weight of glory hidden beneath the dandruff, five o'clock shadow, or nasty temper. That is why C. S. Lewis says:

> It is a serious thing to live in a society of possible gods and goddesses, to remember that the dullest and most uninteresting person you can talk to may one day be a creature which, if you saw it now, you would be strongly tempted to worship, or else a horror and corruption such as you now meet, if it all, only in a nightmare. All day long we are, in some degree, helping each other to one or other of these destinations. It is in the light of these overwhelming possibilities, it is with the awe and the circumspection proper to them, that we should conduct all our dealings with one another, all friendships, all loves, all play, all politics. There are no ordinary people. You have never talked to a mere mortal. Nations, cultures, arts, civilizations — these are mortal, and their life is to ours as the life of a gnat. But it is immortals whom we joke with, work with, marry, snub, and exploit — immortal horrors or everlasting splendors.[3]

And that, in the end, is the point of our search for the different senses of Scripture: not to multiply more and ever more clever footnotes on a biblical passage, nor to fadge up fantasies alien to the text. Rather, it is to learn to see the reality of Christ burning with hidden fire in the heart of his Scripture just as the Spirit of God burned with hidden fire in the heart of the God-Man Christ Jesus. It is to let that fire be kindled in our own souls and, in the light of it, to see the souls of others and set them aflame as well.

---

[3] C. S. Lewis, *The Weight of Glory* (Macmillan: New York, 1980), pp. 18–19.

Scripture has literal and spiritual senses for the same reason that we have bodies and souls. It has an inside and an outside for the same reason we do: because it is a divine *and* a human thing and God has chosen to reveal himself in a human way. And since he has done so, we are now bound to see humans in a new and divine way. God is fond of putting colossal gifts in plain brown wrappers and treasures in jars of clay (2 Corinthians 4:7). The prophet Isaiah says, even of the God-Man himself, "He had no form or comeliness that we should look at him, and no beauty that we should desire him" (Isaiah 53:2). In the same way, Paul tells us, "God chose what is foolish in the world to shame the wise, God chose what is weak in the world to shame the strong, God chose what is low and despised in the world, even things that are not, to bring to nothing things that are" (1 Corinthians 1:27–28).

The proper end of all Scripture study is to obtain our heavenly destiny. To obtain that destiny, we must understand not only what Scripture says, but what the Spirit is saying *through* it. We must see Christ not only when he is shown there (in the literal sense), but even, as he himself insists in Luke 24:25–27, when he is hidden there (in the allegorical sense). We must pattern ourselves upon him in the way that we act (and therefore concern ourselves with discovering the moral sense of Scripture) we must do so in order to ultimately be with Christ where he is, as he prays in John 17:24 (and so fulfill the anagogical sense of Scripture).

For the point of Scripture is not, ultimately, to make us biblical scholars (though that can be handy). It is to make us saints. Our heavenly destiny is to love God and share forever in the rapturous ecstatic love of the Blessed Trinity. And the proper expression of that love is to love one another as he has loved us. The day will come when biblical scholarship, like all knowledge, will be surpassed by something greater than mere knowledge. As St. Paul tells us, "our knowledge is imperfect and our prophecy is imperfect; but when the perfect comes, the imperfect will pass away. When I was a child, I spoke like a child, I thought like a child, I reasoned like a child; when I became a man, I gave up childish ways. For now we see in a mirror dimly, but then face to face. Now I know in part; then I shall understand fully, even as I have been fully understood. So faith, hope, love abide, these three; but the greatest of these is love" (1 Corinthians 13:9–13).

Right now, we are schoolchildren and it is perfectly fitting for us to be studying the Book the Master has given us to read. But there will come a Day, at the consummation of all things, when the school bell will ring and the saints in Christ will close their books, including even the Bible itself, and enter into the greatest and most glorious of all Summer Vacations there ever was. But it would be folly to think that in closing their holy books the saints will have forgotten them. On the contrary, the Scriptures will be closed because, at long last, the saints will remember them all forever. Nor, (peace to the King in *Alice in Wonderland*) will the closing of the holy books of Scripture mean the story has come to an end. Rather, for all the saints in Christ

> it [will be] only the beginning of the real story. All their life in this world and all their adventures . . . [will have] only been the cover and the title page: now at last they [will be] beginning Chapter One of the Great Story, which no one on earth has read: which goes on forever: in which every chapter is better than the one before.[4]

---

[4] C. S. Lewis, *The Last Battle* (Macmillan: New York, 1970), p. 184.

Appendix

Tools For Bible Study

The Holy Bible/Revised Standard Version/Catholic Edition, Ignatius: San Francisco, 1994. A great study bible!

Catechism of the Catholic Church, Bantam: New York, 1995.

The Catechism presents the teaching of Sacred Scripture, the living Tradition in the Church and the authentic Magisterium, as well as the spiritual heritage of the Fathers, Doctors, and saints of the Church.

Medieval Exegesis: The Four Senses of Scripture (Ressourcement) by Henri De Lubac, Mark Sebanc (Translator). Wm. B. Eerdmans Publishing Co.: Grand Rapids, 1998.

An invaluable study of the four senses of Scripture by one of the great Catholic theologians of the twentieth century.

Dictionary of the Bible (John McKenzie, S.J.) Macmillan: New York, 1995.

This volume alphabetically defines words, people and places in the Bible.

Strong's Exhaustive Concordance, Thomas Nelson: Nashville, 1997.

This tool alphabetically lists every word in the Bible with its corresponding scripture reference. Each word is assigned a number which corresponds to the original Hebrew or Greek word indexed in the back of the book. Many other study tools utilize the *Strong's* numbering system.

Theological Wordbook of the Old Testament (Harris, Archer, Waltke) Moody Press: Chicago, 1980.

This two-volume set is great for looking up the meaning of Old Testament words. (Utilizes the *Strong's* numbering system).

The New International Dictionary of New Testament Theology (Colin Brown). Zondervan: Grand Rapids, 1976.

This three-volume set is great for looking up the meaning of New Testament words.

The Moody Atlas of Bible Lands (Barry J. Beitzel). Chicago: Moody Press, 1985.

Some call the land of Israel "the fifth gospel" because it gives the reader another look at God's plan for humanity. The Moody Atlas is an easy-to-use tool with helpful photos as well as various maps covering the Bible lands in different periods of salvation history.

The Faith of the Early Fathers (William A. Jurgens) The Liturgical Press: Collegeville, 1970.

In nearly chronological sequence passages are quoted from the first four centuries of the Christian era. The passages are chosen based on their theological and historical significance, and because they are frequently cited by present day authors.

Navarre Bible: Texts and Commentaries, Four Courts Press: Dublin.

The Navarre Bible is an edition of Sacred Scripture prepared by the Faculty of Theology of Navarre University. Designed for the general reader, it consists of the New Vulgate, the Revised Standard Version, and commentaries. The commentaries provide explanation of the doctrinal and practical meaning of the Scriptural texts, drawing on a rich variety of sources — Church documents, the exegesis of Fathers and Doctors, and the works of prominent spiritual writers.

@ *Home with the Word*

An exciting web-based Bible study series co-authored by Dr. Scott Hahn and Jeff Cavins and available from the Missionaries of Faith web site (*www.moff.org*) on a weekly basis. Materials are easily downloadable and inexpensive ($7.00/month). Perfect for individual or group study of Scripture.

Logos Bible Software 2.0 (St. Joseph Communications, 1-800-526-2151). The *Logos* system comes in a Catholic edition, but you have to specify it.

Recommended Reading

Any Friend of God's Is a Friend of Mine, Patrick Madrid (Basilica Press).

By What Authority? An Evangelical Discovers Tradition, Mark Shea (Our Sunday Visitor).

Catholic for a Reason, Leon Suprenant, Scott Hahn, et al. (Emmaus Road).

A Father Who Keeps His Promises, Scott Hahn (Servant).

The Fathers of the Church, Mike Aquilina (Our Sunday Visitor).

Jesus, Peter & the Keys, David Hess, et al., (Queenship).

Mary and the Fathers of the Church, Luigi Gambero (Ignatius Press).

Not by Scripture Alone, Robert Sungenis, Patrick Madrid, et al. (Queenship).

Pope Fiction: Answers to 30 Myths and Misconceptions About the Papacy, Patrick Madrid (Basilica Press).

Rome Sweet Home, Scott & Kimberly Hahn (Ignatius Press).

Springtime of Evangelization, Pope John Paul II, introduced by Thomas Williams, L.C. (Basilica Press).

Surprised by Truth: 11 Converts Give the Biblical and Historical Reasons for Becoming Catholic, Patrick Madrid (Basilica Press).

Theology and Sanity, Frank Sheed (Ignatius Press).

Theology for Beginners, Frank Sheed (Servant).

Tradition & Traditions, Yves M. J. Congar (Basilica Press).

Upon This Rock, Stephen K. Ray (Ignatius Press).

About the Author

Mark P. Shea is an award-winning lay Catholic writer and speaker for the *Missionaries of Faith Foundation*. In addition to contributing articles to many magazines (including his columns "Heaven and Earth" in *New Covenant* and "The Culture of Life" in *Catholic Parent*), he is the author of *By What Authority?: An Evangelical Discovers Catholic Tradition* (Our Sunday Visitor Books) and *This is My Body: An Evangelical Discovers the Real Presence* (Christendom Press). He has also made numerous guest appearances on both radio and television and has conducted seminars at parishes and conferences throughout the U.S. and abroad. To arrange for him to speak for your parish or conference, contact him at mshea@moff.org. He lives in Washington State with his wife, Janet, and their four sons.

Index

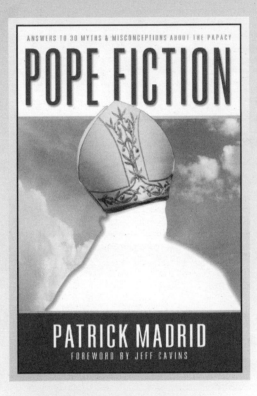

A Homepage for Catholics!

Now there's a website Catholics can turn to for both faith and "whole life" content. Discover CatholicExchange.com.

CatholicExchange.com is the premiere place on the Internet where faith and life converge. Each day we deliver your news, weather and sports alongside bishops' columns, daily Mass readings, Bible studies – even weekly political columns by *CRISIS* publisher Deal Hudson.

Our unique product is sure to make a believer out of you!

We can also build your parish website for free! For information, write to mpinto@catholicexchange.com

Do you know someone whose Catholic Faith ended here?

If you're like most Catholics, your answer is "yes" — a family member, friend, or co-worker.

Now you can do something about it. You can bring them home to the Church with *Envoy* magazine, an exciting bi-monthly journal of Catholic apologetics and evangelization.

Edited by Patrick Madrid, internationally-known Catholic speaker and writer, and editor of the best-selling book *Surprised by Truth*, *Envoy* magazine will teach you how to explain and defend Catholic truth in a way that works. Each issue gives you cutting-edge information and answers from today's top Catholic apologists, evangelists, and writers. Our articles are consistently fresh, upbeat, useful, and *charitable*.

Envoy magazine will show you how to explain your Catholic Faith intelligently, defend it charitably, and share it *effectively* — it will prepare you to be an ambassador for Christ.

Subscribe today, and the next time you're faced with friends or loved ones who have lost their Catholic Faith (if not their First Communion picture), you can answer their questions and be a light to guide them home.

To Subscribe Call 1-800-55ENVOY

Bringing Christ to the World

www.envoymagazine.com